Learn ASP.NET Core MVC

Be ready next week using Visual Studio 2017

Arnaud Weil

Learn ASP.NET Core MVC

Be ready next week using Visual Studio 2017

Arnaud Weil

ISBN 978-0-244-61234-4

To my wonderful kids. Your love and support fueled this book.

To my parents for teaching me freedom and making sure I can enjoy it.

To the great people that made and make the Web a fantastic platform for content and application delivery.

Contents

Introduction   i
    What this book is not   i
    Prerequisites   i
    How to read this book   ii
    Tools you need   ii
    Source code   iii

1. Why ASP.NET Core ?   1
    1.1 What is it ?   1
    1.2 Why use it ?   1
    1.3 Competing technologies   2

2. ASP.NET Core at its simplest   5
    2.1 Setting up the server   5
    2.2 Very basic Startup configuration   6
    2.3 Barebone configuration   7
    2.4 ASP.NET MVC comes in   9

3. Creating our Web Site   11
    3.1 Visual Studio scaffolding   11
    3.2 Quick facts about that template   16

4. ASP.NET MVC inner workings **17**
   4.1 Principles 17
   4.2 View 18
   4.3 Bootstrap 20
   4.4 Controller 21
   4.5 It's your turn to code: do-it-yourself . . . 23
   4.6 Exercise - Create the application 25
   4.7 Exercise solution 26

5. Razor **29**
   5.1 Razor syntax 29
   5.2 Exercise - Add code to the home page . . 33
   5.3 Exercise solution 34
   5.4 Layout views 34
   5.5 Exercise - Remove some links 41
   5.6 Exercise solution 41
   5.7 Helpers 42
   5.8 Partial views 44

6. Understanding ASP.NET MVC **45**
   6.1 Flashback 45
   6.2 Routing 46
   6.3 Controllers 48
   6.4 Be lazy 53
   6.5 Let's go all the way 56

7. Typing things up **61**
   7.1 The problem with ViewBag and ViewData 61
   7.2 Using and typing the model 61
   7.3 Conventions and simplicity: introducing
        the ViewModel 64

8. Dependency Injection (DI) **71**

  8.1 DI steps 71

  8.2 Services registration 72

  8.3 Getting services through injection 75

  8.4 Extension methods for dependency injection 77

  8.5 Wrapping it up 77

9. Entity Framework Core models **81**

  9.1 Exercise - Create the Product model and DbContext 91

  9.2 Exercise solution 91

  9.3 Exercise - Add code that creates a database with some products 94

  9.4 Exercise solution 94

  9.5 Exercise - Display a products list 98

  9.6 Exercise solution 98

10. Updating server data **103**

  10.1 Action parameters 103

  10.2 Word of caution about URLs 105

  10.3 Exercise - Display product details 107

  10.4 Exercise solution 108

  10.5 HTTP Post parameters 109

  10.6 Passing a full blown object 111

  10.7 Sit and watch - Basic product calculator . 113

  10.8 Exercise - Add a search box to the products list 118

  10.9 Exercise solution 118

11. Updating data scenario **121**

11.1 Steps 121
11.2 Controller 121
11.3 Automated generation of controller and views 123
11.4 Exercise - Create the products management back-office 127
11.5 Exercise solution - Create the products management back-office 127

12. Doing more with controllers and actions . . . **131**
12.1 Actions can generate more than views . . 131
12.2 Exercise - Add images to the products . . 135
12.3 Exercise solution - Add images to the products 136
12.4 Input validation 138

13. Basic security **143**
13.1 Preventing Cross-Site Scripting 143
13.2 Rejecting extra fields 145
13.3 Authenticating users 146
13.4 Exercise - Secure the back-office 147
13.5 Exercise solution - Secure the back-office 148

14. State management **149**
14.1 State stores 149
14.2 Session state 150
14.3 Exercise - Add products to a basket . . . 153
14.4 Exercise solution - Add products to a basket 154
14.5 Exercise - Basket contents 159
14.6 Exercise solution - Basket contents 159

15. Web API **163**

15.1 Use cases 163
15.2 Creating an API is simple 164
15.3 API results format 165

16. Going further **167**
16.1 Creating Razor helpers 167
16.2 Display and edit templates 168

Definitions **171**
Dynamic object 171
Entity Framework 171
Project 172
Solution 172
Solution Explorer 172

A word from the author **173**

The Learn collection **175**

Introduction

What this book is not

I made my best to keep this book small, so that you can learn ASP.NET Core quickly without getting lost in petty details. If you are looking for a reference book where you'll find answers to all the questions you may have within the next 4 years of your ASP.NET Core practice, you'll find other heavy books for that.

My purpose is to swiftly provide you with the tools you need to code your first ASP.NET Core application and be able to look for more by yourself when needed. While some authors seem to pride themselves in having the thickest book, in this series I'm glad I achieved the thinnest possible book for my purpose. Though I tried my best to keep all of what seems necessary, based on my 15 years experience of teaching .NET.

I assume that you know what ASP.NET MVC is and when to use it. In case you don't, read the following *What is ASP.NET Core* chapter.

Prerequisites

In order for this book to meet its goals, you must :

- Have basic experience creating applications with C#
- Have working knowledge of HTML
- Know what a Web application is

How to read this book

This book's aim is to make you productive as quickly as possible. For this we'll use some theory, several demonstrations, plus exercises. Exercises appear like the following:

 Do it yourself: Time to grab your keyboard and code away to meet the given objectives.

Tools you need

The only tool you'll need to work through that book is Visual Studio 2017. You can get any of those editions:

- Visual Studio 2017 Community (free)
- Visual Studio 2017 Professional or Entreprise

When installing Visual Studio, make sure you select the *ASP.NET* and *.NET Core* components.

Source code

All of the source code for the demos and do-it-yourself solutions is available at https://bitbucket.org/epobb/aspnetcoreexercises

It can be downloaded as a ZIP file[1], or if you installed GIT you can simply type:

```
git clone https://bitbucket.org/epobb/aspnetcoreexerc\
ises.git
```

---

[1] https://bitbucket.org/epobb/aspnetcoreexercises/downloads

1. Why ASP.NET Core ?

If you're in a hurry, you can safely skip this chapter and head straight to the Creating our Web Site chapter. This *Why ASP.NET Core* chapter is there for those that want to know why ASP.NET Core should be used.

1.1 What is it ?

In a nutshell, ASP.NET Core is a technology used to create Web applications.

Web applications are used with a browser. Examples of Web applications are Facebook, Google, and in fact most of the services you use. When you enter an `http://something` url in your browser, you get a Web application.

Simply put, ASP.NET Core can be used to create a Web application like Facebook. Or a store, which is what we do in this book's exercises.

1.2 Why use it ?

In case you know .NET and need to create a Web application, using ASP.NET makes sense since you can reuse your knowledge of the .NET Framework (or .NET Core) and language abilities (like C# and VB.NET).

At this time, there are two versions of ASP.NET:

- ASP.NET 4.6, using the .NET Framework 4.6.
- ASP.NET Core.

ASP.NET 4.6 is the legacy version coming all the way from the year 2001. It is full of features but should be used mostly when porting existing .NET code, since the .NET Core platform doesn't have all of the classes that where available in .NET. However, ASP.NET 4.6 is limited to running on Windows platforms.

ASP.NET Core should be considered for new projects. It is cross-platform (Windows, Linux, OS-X, Docker), scalable and efficient. This book is about ASP.NET Core.

ASP.NET Core can be used to produce APIs and HTML pages out of the box. In order to render HTML, it sports an MVC middleware which we'll learn in this book.

1.3 Competing technologies

There are many technology stacks used to create Web applications. On a technological standpoint the following stacks would for instance allow to develop applications in a way similar to ASP.NET Core :

- Node.JS + Express
- Ruby on Rails
- Meteor

Selecting one technology or another can be debated for a while. It often boils down to beliefs or preferences, but there can be good reasons. For instance, if you know JavaScript and HTTP but nothing about .NET, you'll probably get an easier time with Node.JS + Express than with ASP.NET Core.

2. ASP.NET Core at its simplest

Before I introduce ASP.NET MVC, I'd like to show you that ASP.NET Core can run with a minimalist setup. Two classes are needed: *Program* and *Startup*.

2.1 Setting up the server

We need to create a server instance. It's the object that will serve the HTTP requests. Kestrel is such a server and is included with ASP.NET Core. We can run it using the following code:

```
public class Program
{
  public static void Main(string[] args)
  {
    var host = new WebHostBuilder()
      .UseKestrel()
      .UseStartup<Startup>()
      .Build();

    host.Run();
  }
}
```

Note that this code references a *Startup* class. We need to provide that class.

> With such code, our application is hosted inside a console host, but we can easily get good integration with IIS, Apache or NGINX should our needs grow later. The code example below shows the change needed in the *Main* method in order to run under IIS.

Hosting the application in IIS

```
var host = new WebHostBuilder()
  .UseKestrel()
  .UseIISIntegration()
  .Build();
```

2.2 Very basic Startup configuration

The following code creates a minimalist setup.

```
public class Startup
{
  public void Configure(IApplicationBuilder app)
  {
    app.UseWelcomePage();
  }
}
```

Using that code and the *Program* class above, we already have a Web server. It provides users with a page about ASP.NET Core:

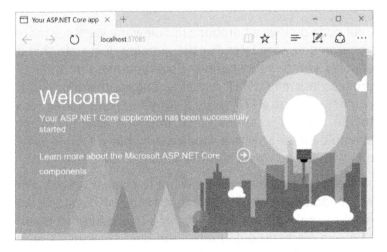

2.3 Barebone configuration

Should we want to get to the bare metal of ASP.NET Core, we can replace the above *Startup* class with the following one:

```
public class Startup
{
  public void Configure(IApplicationBuilder app)
  {
    app.Run(async (context) =>
    {
      await context.Response
        .WriteAsync("Hello World!");
    });
  }
}
```

That code defines a barebone middleware. We'll see more about middleware later. For the moment, just note that it enables you to run whatever code you need in order to process incoming HTTP requests. The *context* parameter you get when an HTTP request comes in gives you access to the request, response, and anything related. In my example I answer with a simple string but we could write any Web server application by adding code there.

At that very moment you may want to close this book. For any middle-size application that mode of development would simply grow into something impossible to maintain. I'm glad you didn't close the book, because I have good news: ASP.NET Core offers a middleware that makes it easy to write a maintainable, testable Web application: ASP.NET MVC. Just read on.

2.4 ASP.NET MVC comes in

ASP.NET is a flexible middleware made for creating HTML and API web applications. It provides for a well made separation of concerns and even offers dependency injection support out of the box. Using it is as simple as adding a line to our Startup class:

```
app.UseMvc()
```

But we won't even need to manually add that line. Visual Studio 2017 is part of our toolbelt, so let's start using it.

3. Creating our Web Site

3.1 Visual Studio scaffolding

In order to create an ASP.NET Core Application, I can simply start Visual Studio 2017 and select *File / New / Project* from the menu. I know *New Web Site* sounds tempting but don't use it, that kind of site doesn't scale up well once you get to real applications.

I'm taken to the *New project* dialog box. From the left menu I'll select *Visual C#* since it's the most common coding language for .NET, then *Web*. In the middle pane I'll select *ASP.NET Core Web Application (.NET Core)*. In the lower part of the dialog box, next to the *Name:* label I'll type the name of my project: Demos.

Now I click the *OK* button and I'm taken to a second dialog: *New ASP.NET Core Web Application (.NET Core)*. Time to select the features we want. I'll select *Web Application*, make sure the *Enable Docker Support* checkbox is unchecked and authentication is set to *Individual User Accounts* (if necessary, click the *Change Authentication* button to select that option). Here's what that dialog looks like:

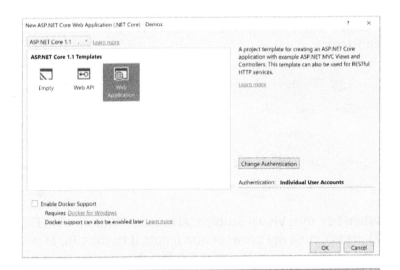

Just a word about the other options, in case you wonder. *Enable Docker Support* can be unchecked, because it's easy to add Docker support later on when we need it. Having the *Authentication: Individual User Accounts* ensures that it's dead-easy to get a local database (or SQL Server with one easy change) based authentication for my application. As far as templates are concerned, *Web Application* just ensures we get starter files created for us by Visual Studio; in any case we could select any of the three templates and add MVC or API support in a breeze.

Now I click the *OK* button of the *New ASP.NET Core Web Application* dialog and that's it for now: my application is ready. In order to run it inside my browser, I'll select

Debug / Start Debugging from the menu, or use the *F5* shortcut:

When I do this, Visual Studio starts a local Web server (IIS Express), runs my browser and points it to the URL of my site on that server, then finally attaches to the running code in *debug* mode so that it can catch any exception or show the code when I reach a breakpoint.

This is what I get in my browser:

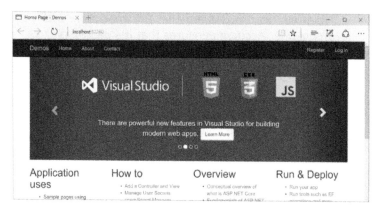

What's nice is that the site is responsive (the default template uses Boostrap):

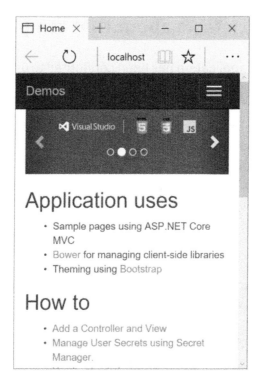

That application also has a menu above, with links that take me to almost empty "About" and "Contact" pages. Also note that we already have fully-functional "Log in" and "Register" links for user authentication. If I use them, a local SQL Server database will be created for storage.

Well, we have kind of a nice startup after just a few clicks. Now let's see some theory before we can extend our application. Don't worry, I'll keep it short: this book focuses on getting you up and running quickly.

3.2 Quick facts about that template

This basic application has been configured to use ASP.NET MVC. In short, MVC allows for:

- Separation of concerns: *controllers* handle the HTTP request while *views* generate the outgoing HTML.
- Testability (easy unit testing of the controllers).

Several folders have been created as part of that initial scaffolding. We'll see more about them through the book; in short:

- wwwroot: content that will be available to the client (browser);
- Data: Entity Framework classes;
- Model: business classes;
- Services: dependencies that will be injected;
- Models: MVC models;
- Views: MVC views;
- Controllers: MVC controllers.

4. ASP.NET MVC inner workings

4.1 Principles

When our browser queries an ASP.NET MVC URL, there are three elements that work together in order to produce an HTML page:

- A *View* produces the HTML;
- A *Controller*:
    - fetches the data and provides it to the view
    - selects the view
- A *Route* selects the controller.

That's an easy process. Here's a schema of it:

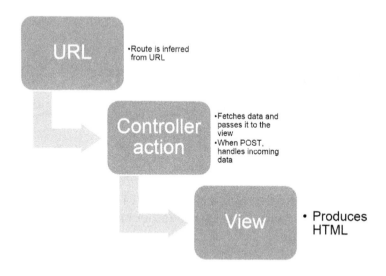

4.2 View

Once inferred from the URL, the view is looked for into the following paths:

- Views/[Controller]/[Action].cshtml
- Views/Shared

When coding the view, the Razor syntax is used. It's a concise view language crafted specifically for ASP.NET MVC.

Before we begin learning about the Razor syntax, we're going to have a look at what's part of the Visual Studio template that was created.

Let's take a look at the project structure. For this I'll use the Solution Explorer.

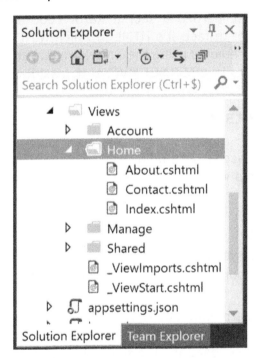

You can see that there is a "Views" folder containing a "Home" sub-folder, inside of which there is an "Index.cshtml" file. As seen above, when ASP.NET MVC looks for the view corresponding to the "Index" action of the "Home" controller, it will get that Views\Home\Index.cshtml file. Sound abrupt? Bear with me.

Let's open the Views\Home\Index.cshtml file. Apart from the first 3 lines, it contains pure HTML markup. That markup will be rendered to the browser. And it is also Razor code.

So you just learned a secret: Razor code is basically HTML code. In fact, it's HTML in which we'll add some special statements using the @ mark. Yeah, I know you're beginning to love ASP.NET MVC, or at least Razor.

4.3 Bootstrap

The codebase Visual Studio just scaffolded includes Bootstrap. It's a widely used client-side JavaScript and CSS framework that offers:

- Styles
- Grid system for responsive pages creation
- Components: navbar, carousel and more

You can learn more about Bootstrap on its page[1]. I just want to tell you about the responsive Bootstrap classes so that you understand the scaffolded code.

Bootstrap divides the available width into lines of 12 columns. When you create a zone, you can define how many columns it takes using classes like col-md-3. Depending on exact name used, the specified amount of columns applies to different screen sizes:

- col-lg-N for pages 1200 pixels or wider

---

[1] http://getbootstrap.com

- col-md-N for pages 992 pixels or wider
- col-sm-N for pages 768 pixels or wider
- col-xs-N for page widths smaller than 768 pixels

Since an example is worth a thousand words:

```
<div class="row">
  <div class="col-md-6 col-sm-3">
    50% of the width on wide screens
    25% of the width on small screens
  </div>
  <div class="col-md-6 col-sm-9">
    50% of the width on wide screens
    75% of the width on small screens
  </div>
</div>
```

Using the example above, you get:

- 1/2 and 1/2 blocks on pages 992 pixels or wider
- 1/4 and 3/4 blocks on pages between 768 and 992 pixels
- two full-width blocks on smaller pages

4.4 Controller

Inside the solution, we can also find a `Controllers\HomeController.cs` file. Let's open that file.

```
public class HomeController : Controller
{
  public IActionResult Index()
  {
    return View();
  }

  // ...
}
```

You can see that the class is named *HomeController*, and it contains a public method named *Index*. When ASP.NET looks for the view corresponding to the "Index" action of the "Home" controller, it will get this method.

The "Index" method contains a simple `return View();` statement. It means that the default view should be returned for that action.

We're almost there. Now let's have a look at the `Startup.cs` file. It contains the following code:

```
routes.MapRoute(
  name: "default",
  template: "{controller=Home}/{action=Index}/{id?}"
);
```

This is the routing configuration. As of now this is the only line, but you may add as many as you wish here.

See the *template* property? It states how ASP.NET MVC will parse incoming URLs. What it means is that if some-one types the `http://mysite/home/index` URL in their browser

ASP.NET will invoke the Index action from the Home controller. It also states that if someone types the http://mysite URL in their browser ASP.NET will invoke the Index action from the Home controller because they are the defaults.

Got it? Now let's sum up what happens for a sample request:

1. Someone types http://mysite/home/index in their browser.
2. ASP.NET MVC understands it has to look for the Index action from the Home controller, so it invokes the Index method from the HomeController class.
3. The return View(); statement means the ASP.NET needs to return the default view.
4. ASP.NET fetches the Views\Home\Index.cshtml file and renders it to the browser. It contains HTML which can be enhanced using the Razor syntax for server-side generation.

Easy, isn't it? Well that's almost all there is to ASP.NET MVC. Read those four steps again until you get them right, because they are the backbone of the MVC process.

Time to put in practice all of that stuff you just learned. And I bet your fingers are itchy for coding.

4.5 It's your turn to code: do-it-yourself

Now is your turn to grab the keyboard and code away. Oh, just let me explain you how that works, in case you're not familiar with my *Learn collection* books.

About exercises in this book

All of the exercises are linked together: you're going to build a small e-commerce application. You'll allow users to browse through your products, add them to their basket, and you'll also create a full back-end where the site administrators will be able to list, create, modify, and delete products.

In case you get stuck

You should be able to solve each exercise all by yourself. If you get stuck or don't have a computer at hand (or you don't have the prerequisites for that book, which is fine with me!), no problem. I'll provide the solution for all of the exercises in this book, right after each of them.

4.6 Exercise - Create the application

Create a new ASP.NET Core application project using MVC. Ensure that authentication will be done using accounts from a database (that's the default option).

Change the home page so that it displays a welcome message and a "Startup" section. As a result it should look like the following:

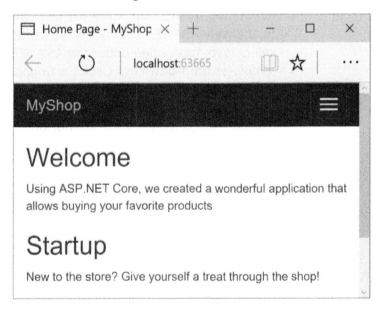

I know, it's basic, but you need to learn some more things before you can do more.

4.7 Exercise solution

- Open Visual Studio.
- Click on the *File / New / Project...* menu entry.
- In the *New Project* dialog, select the *Installed* tab on the left. Select *Templates / Visual C# / Web* on the left. In the center, select *ASP.NET Core Web Application (.NET Core)*. At the bottom, type MyShop next to the *Name:* label. Click the *OK* button.
- In the *New ASP.NET Core Web Application* dialog, select *Web Application* under the *ASP.NET Core 1.1 templates* drop-down list. Click the *Change Authentication* button.
- In the *Change Authentication* dialog, select *Individual User Accounts*. Click the *OK* button.
- Back in the *New ASP.NET Core Web Application* dialog, click the *OK* button.
- In the *Solution Explorer* (on the right-hand side), open the *Views* folder, then the *Home* folder located underneath.
- Double-click the *Index.cshtml* file.
- Locate the following code:

```
<div id="myCarousel" ...>
  ...
</div>

<div class="row">
    <div class="col-md-3">
      ...
    </div>
</div>
```

- Replace that code with the following one :

```
<div class="col-md-3">
  <h2>Welcome</h2>
  <p>
    Using ASP.NET Core, we created a wonderful
    application that allows buying your
    favorite products
  </p>
</div>
<div class="col-md-3">
  <h2>Startup</h2>
  <p>
    New to the store? Give yourself a treat
    through the shop!
  </p>
</div>
```

- Click the *Build / Build Solution* menu.

- Run the application: click the *Debug / Start Debugging* menu.

5. Razor

5.1 Razor syntax

A view contains HTML code that is parsed and rendered on the client side. That is, in the browser. You need a way to generate that HTML dynamically according to server-side data. For instance, authorization data fetched from a database. This is what Razor is used for. The Razor syntax augments your view's HTML with server-side capabilities.

Razor is a clean, concise syntax that enables you to pour C# throughout your HTML. That is, server-side C# throughout the client-side HTML.

No closing tags when they can be guessed.

Consider the following example using Razor:

```
<div>
  Hello @userName, check your
  <a href="/email?id=@userId">
    e-mail
  </a>
</div>
```

Most of it is plain HTML. The only C# parts are userName and userId. All we need to do is place a @ symbol in front

of them and they will be replaced on the server side with
the actual value of these variables.

HTML and C# blend smoothly

In order to get a seamless integration between HTML and
C#, the Razor parser behaves roughly as:

1. Code is supposed to be HTML
2. When the @ symbol is encountered, code is supposed to be C# afterwards until the end of the C#
   expression
3. When an opening bracket { is encountered, code
   is supposed to be C# afterwards until the closing
   bracket } or an opening HTML tag is encountered

In the following example, note how HTML and C# play
nicely together using the Razor syntax:

```
1   <ul>
2     @foreach (var product in Model) {
3       <li>@product.Name</li>
4     }
5   </ul>
```

Syntactically, the Razor parser can infer that lines 1 and
5 are HTML while lines 2 and 4 are C#. Likewise, it can
infer that line 3 is an HTML element containing C#.

Conditions

As we saw, end of instructions are implicitly detected in Razor. Notice there is no closing @ in the following example:

```
<div>
  <h1>Welcome</h1>
  @if(User.Indentity.IsAuthenticated) {
    <div>You are @User.Identity.Name, hello!</div>
  }
  else {
    <div>Please <a href="...">log-in</a></div>
  }
</div>
```

Multiline code

Use @{ ... } when your code is multiline:

```
@{
  var isAutenticated = User.Indentity.IsAuthenticated;
  var userName = User.Identity.Name;
}
<div>
  <h1>Welcome</h1>
  @if(isAuthenticated) {
    <div>You are @userName, hello!</div>
  }
  else {
```

```
    <div>Please <a href="...">log in</a></div>
  }
</div>
```

You can place any block of C# code in your view using that syntax.

You might as well fetch your whole data from a database or API in such a block, apply functional logic, and create your whole application like that. Which means you might close that book and shout "I know ASP.NET MVC !".

I don't recommend you to do so, though: doing so mixes code and presentation, plus it makes the view responsible for fetching its data and applying functional logic. Which goes against SOC (Separation of concerns). Keep reading on, and you'll make the difference between a hobby programmer and a professional one.

5.2 Exercise - Add code to the home page

Display the next delivery schedule on the home page. Since we want to keep it basic, just use the following logic: next delivery will be tomorrow at 9 am. Make sure the date is explicitly displayed.

The resulting page should look like the following:

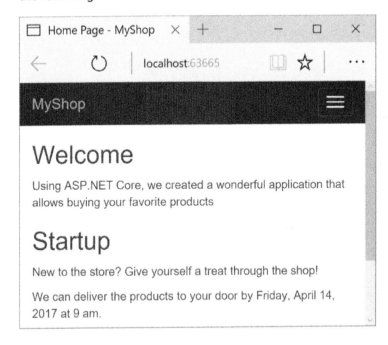

5.3 Exercise solution

- Open the `Views/Home/Index.cshtml` file.
- Locate the following code

```
<p>
  New to the store? Give yourself a treat
  through the shop!
</p>
```

- Replace it with the following one :

```
<p>
  New to the store? Give yourself a treat
  through the shop!
</p>
<p>
    We can deliver the products to your door
    by @DateTime.Now.AddDays(1).ToString("D") at 9 am.
</p>
```

5.4 Layout views

Many times you want the same HTML tags to appear on every page of your application. Think about a navigation menu or page footer. Instead of repeating it, you can simply refer to a layout view from another view.

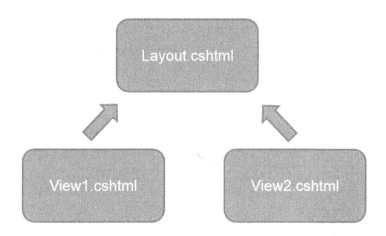

Basic layout

In the simplest case, here's the code you can use in your layout and view:

Layout.cshtml

```
<html>
  <head>...</head>
  <body>
    <div class="content">
      @RenderBody()
    </div>
  </body>
</html>
```

View.cshtml → *only rendered*

```
@{
    Layout = "Layout.cshtml";
}
<p>
    This message will go in the "RenderBody"
    part of the layout.
</p>
```

A layout view like `Layout.cshtml` is never rendered directly from an action. Instead, an action may return `View.cshtml`. As you can see, `View.cshtml` refers to `Layout.cshtml`. That's how ASP.NET knows that it should merge your view into its layout.

In the `Layout.cshtml` file, there is a `RenderBody` statement. It tells ASP.NET to insert here all of the content of the view that is not part of a *section*. We have no section defined in our view, so our whole view is rendered where the `RenderBody` statement appears.

I know you wonder what sections are. We're going to see them in a few minutes. Just to be clear, the HTML that will be rendered by ASP.NET when `View.cshtml` needs to be rendered will be the following:

What's rendered by ASP.NET

```
<html>
  <head>...</head>
  <body>
    <div class="content">
      <p>
        This message will go in the "RenderBody"
        part of the layout.
      </p>
    </div>
  </body>
</html>
```

Alright, as you can see Razor's layout system is dead-easy. Let's see some more.

Layout using sections

In most cases though, you want disparate chunks of your pages to be common, not just the header and footer. That's when you use sections. Sections allow for a layout to specify which parts may be customized by a view, marking them optional as needed.

Consider the following example layout and view:

Layout.cshtml

```
<html>
  <head>...</head>
  <body>
    <div class="header">
      @RenderSection("top", optional:true)
    </div>
    <div class="content">
      @RenderBody()
    </div>
    <div class="footer">
      @RenderSection("bottom", optional:true)
    </div>
  </body>
</html>
```

position based?

View.cshtml ← *what gets rendered*

```
@{
  Layout = "Layout.cshtml";
}
<p>
  This message will go in the "RenderBody"
  part of the layout.
</p>

@section top {
  <h1>Some title</h1>
}
```

should say "bottom"?

```
@section footer {
    <p>Copyright us</p>
}
```

Now guess what the final rendered HTML will look like?

```
<html>
  <head>...</head>
  <body>
    <div class="header">
       <h1>Some title</h1>
    </div>
    <div class="content">
      <p>
        This message will go in the "RenderBody"
        part of the layout.
      </p>
    </div>
    <div class="footer">
      <p>Copyright us</p>
    </div>
  </body>
</html>
```

Note that the `optional: true` statements allow for a view not to include a specific section. In our example, `View.cshtml` might as well have missed a `@section top` and this section would have been empty. In case your layout states `optional: false` and that section is missing from the view, rendering the view will result in an exception.

Location of the layout

When ASP.NET MVC looks for a view or layout, it looks into the Views\Shared folder as we saw earlier. Since a layout is a shared file, best practice is to place it in the Views\Shared folder. As a matter of fact, if you look at that folder in your solution, you'll find a _Layout.cshtml file that is your common layout.

DRY

You surely know that a best coding practice is *DRY* or *Do not Repeat Yourself*. That's what layouts are about. But why would we include the following lines at the top of most of our views?

```
@{
    Layout = "Layout.cshtml";
}
```

In fact, if you look at your Views\Home\Index.cshml you'll see it doesn't include such a statement, though it does use Views\Shared_Layout.cshtml for final rendering.

There's no magic in that. If you look again it your Views folder, you'll see there's a _ViewStart.cshtml file. ASP.NET MVC automatically applies any _ViewStart.cshtml file to all of the views inside its folder and subfolders. Since we have a Views_ViewStart.cshtml file, it will apply to all of our views. If we open that file, we can see that it contains the following code:

```
@{
   Layout = "_Layout";
}
```

Bingo! That's why every view will use Shared/_Layout.cshtml as a layout. Of course, if you want another layout for a particular view, you can set the Layout property to another value, or even *null* in case you want no layout. Any property set in a view will override the ones set in _Layout.cshtml.

Good, now you know where most files of an ASP.NET Core MVC project are located. Time to check your skills with some practice.

5.5 Exercise - Remove some links

 Currently, your home page and all of the pages contain links to "About" and "Contact" views in their header menu. Remove those two links.

5.6 Exercise solution

- Open the Views/Shared/_Layout.cshtml file.
- Locate and delete the following lines of code :

```
<li><a asp-area="" asp-controller="Home"
  asp-action="About">About</a></li>
<li><a asp-area="" asp-controller="Home"
  asp-action="Contact">Contact</a></li>
```

5.7 Helpers → not 100% sure

In C#, when you need to factorize similar pieces of code that have small variations, you can write parameterized methods. Well we have just that in Razor, and they are called *helpers*. Helpers are invoked like methods - that is, with parameters - and produce HTML.

We'll see later in this book how to create your own helpers (see here) using C# or the Razor syntax itself. For now, it'll be enough to know that ASP.NET MVC offers ready-to-use helpers.

Here are some of the helpers readily available:

```
@Url.Content("~/relativePath/willBeConverted.jpg")
```

This one will generate an absolute URL, whatever the base URL of your application. A typical use could be for an image or link URL:

```
<img src='@Url.Content("~/relativePath/willBeConverte\
d.jpg")' />
```

And here's one that will generate a single-choice list using a collection you provide it.

```
@Html.ListBox("name", enumerableList)
```

A very common one too, used to generate a link (the `<a/>` HTML element) to one of your actions:

```
@Html.ActionLink(label, actionName, controllerName)
```

What's neat about it is that you don't reference a URL. Instead, the URL will be generated using those parameters. Which means that if your routing configuration changes (e.g. for SEO purposes), you won't need to change any Html.ActionLink parameters.

As stated earlier, since Razor allows you to place any block of code in a view using the `@{ ... }` syntax, you might think you are ready to code your application. However, there are many things you may want to do for a view to render:

- Taking into account any HTTP POST values coming from a form.
- Manage connection to data sources (databases, APIs and the like).
- Apply functional logic

ASP.NET Core MVC allows you to do all of this in a neat, separated way. So please refrain yourself from coding all of this in your view, and read on. Let's learn how to do this in a professional way.

5.8 Partial views

When a common HTML base should be shared amongst views, layout views may not be the right answer. For instance, when only a small block is shared, not the wrapping layout of views. In that case, partial views allow for view code sharing just like layouts.

Partial views are declared like standard views; they can be reused in any view. There is a helper for injecting a partial view inside your view.

In case the view to be injected has no action, just use the `Html.Partial` helper. You can provide it with a view name and optionally a model (more about models later):

```
@Html.Partial("SameFolder")

@Html.Partial("/Views/Folder/MyView.cshtml")

@Html.Partial("SameFolder", viewModel)
```

6. Understanding ASP.NET MVC

6.1 Flashback

A quick reminder about the ASP.NET MVC process before we move on:

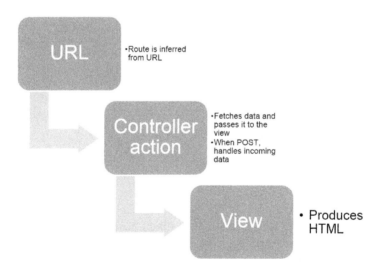

We used that schema before, but it should make more sense now that you saw what a route, a controller and a view are. We're going to dive deeper into those concepts,

and apply them to creating our application in a professional way.

6.2 Routing

As we saw earlier, a routing engine is in charge of parsing
the incoming request's URL and inferring which controller
and action to invoke. Practically, an action is a method
inside a class (the controller).

There is no magic. The Program.cs file contains the following code:

```
public class Program
{
  public static void Main(string[] args)
  {
    ...
    .UseStartup<Startup>()
    ...
  }
}
```

Which means that the Startup class contains application
configuration code. In turn, the Startup class contains the
following code:

```
app.UseMvc(routes =>
{
  routes.MapRoute(
    name: "default",
    template: "{controller=Home}/{action=Index}/{id?}"
  );
});
```

Sounds familiar? That's because we saw it earlier. This is the only place of code that decides how to convert an incoming URL into an action and controller. In one place we state that we want to use the MVC engine as part of the middleware that handle incoming requests and configure its routing rules.

As we saw earlier, what `url: "{controller}/{action}/{id}"` means is that if someone types the `http://mysite/home/index` URL in their browser ASP.NET MVC will invoke the `Index` action from the `Home` controller.

Best of all is that if we change the routing configuration, we don't need to impact the remainder of our application as long as we used the `Html.Action(label, actionName, controllerName)` helper in our views (we saw that in the helpers section).

Let's suppose that we have a ShowProductDetails action in our Products controller, and an ice-cream product which was assigned and ID of 469. With the default route, it should be invoked with the following URL:

```
http://mysite/Products/ShowProductDetails/469
```

Not that great for search-engine-optimization and URL-friendliness. So we might add the following code to our MapRoute method:

```
routes.MapRoute(
    name: "ProductSEO",
    template: "{name}/{id}-Details",
    defaults: new { controller = "Products", action = "\
ShowProductDetails" }
);
```

Thanks to that new route, a user can now type in the following URL:

```
http://mysite/ice-cream/469-Details
```

That's a much friendlier URL, plus my ice-cream will be better indexed by search engines when someone searches for an ice-cream since its name appears in the URL.

Even better: the `http://mysite/Products/ShowProductDetails/469` URL is also still valid since we didn't remove the default route (but we may choose to remove it if needed).

6.3 Controllers

A controller's duty

A controller:

1. Handles the incoming HTTP request and provides a response.
2. Is made of actions.
3. Contains the business logic (or calls to the business logic).
4. Can be unit-tested since it doesn't reference properties of a view.

Anatomy of a controller

Writing a controller is simple: each action is a public method returning an *IActionResult*, and actions are placed inside a public class whose name is suffixed with *Controller* and inherits from the `Microsoft.AspNetCore.Mvc.Controller` class.

```
public class ProductsController : Controller
{
    public IActionResult Action1()
    {
        ...
    }
}
```

According to the default route, this *Action1* action could be invoked using the following URL:

```
http://mysite/Products/Action1
```
an action

ActionResult

A controller can return:

- a view, which produces HTML
- whatever content (JSON, image, and so on)

What you return goes back in the HTTP response. Usually you return a view for a browser to render the HTML, but it can really be anything. When you want to return a view, the base `Microsoft.AspNetCore.Mvc.Controller` class offers a `View` method. Should you call it without any parameter, it will return the default view for your action, without passing it any model (more on that later). Look at the following basic code for an action:

```
public class ProductsController : Controller
{
    public IActionResult SayHello()
    {
        return View();
    }
}
```

This instructs ASP.NET MVC to return the *SayHello* view. ASP.NET MVC will look for that view in the following locations:

- Views/Products/SayHello.cshtml
- Views/Shared/SayHello.cshtml

You'll be glad to hear that, like most parts of ASP.NET, this search pattern can be changed. Even better: ASP.NET MVC is highly modular and allows you to fetch a view from anywhere you like: a database or even another web server. But that's another story and you likely do not need such advanced functionality.

IActionResult can be more than a view

You surely noticed that all of our action methods specify `IActionResult` as their return type. Up to now we called the `View()` method from our base `Controller` class, which returns a `ViewResult`.

The `ViewResult` class inherits from the `ActionResult` abstract class that implements the `IActionResult` interface. Many other classes do so, which allows you to return a whole lot of different content for your action, not just a view. Here are some of the types that implement `IActionResult`:

- ContentResult
- FileContentResult
- JsonResult
- NotFoundResult
- NoContentResult
- OkResult

- PartialViewResult
- PhysicalFileResult
- RedirectResult
- RedirectToActionResult
- RedirectToRouteResult
- UnauthorizedResult
- ViewResult

I won't go into an enumeration of those types, since their names almost state it all, plus the MSDN documentation is good enough as a reference. Of interest is the fact that they represent information for several parts of the HTTP response. For instance, NotFoundResult means a 404 error code, while JsonResult means a 200 code, an `application/json` content type and holds the body of the HTTP response (JSON, needless to say). Please bear with me, and we'll use several of those types later on.

Passing data from the Controller to the View

As you already learned, ASP.NET MVC will invoke a controller which in most cases will return a view. Since the view produces HTML, it is very likely to contain data (formatted as HTML). We saw that a good practice is for the controller to fetch the data, so we need some way for the controller to pass data to the view. Good news: there are several ways to do this.

A first, a loosely coupled and loose way to do this is to use either `ViewData` or `ViewBag`. They both are a dictionary (keyed values) of objects to pass from the controller to the view. ViewData and ViewBag only differ in the way they are accessed.

Here's how you add data to them (in the controller):

```
ViewData["message"] = ...;
ViewBag.message = ...;
```

And here's how you fetch data from them (in the view):

```
<p>This is a message: @ViewData["message"]<p>
<p>And the same message @ViewBag.message</p>
```

Which one to use then? It simply depends on your tastes, since they offer the same functionality. It's just a syntactic difference between those twins: ViewData is a *dictionary* while ViewBag is a dynamic object.

6.4 Be lazy

A very common task is to create an action which returns a view. Basic creation of an action is a quick task, and you'll be glad to know that Visual Studio helps us create the corresponding view in a few clicks instead of navigating the Solution Explorer and reminding of the conventions. Let me show you.

Let's say we just added Action1 to our Products controller

```
public class ProductsController : Controller
{
  public IActionResult Action1()
  {
    ...
    return View();
  }
}
```

All we have to do is right-click on the `Action1` method. Visual Studio shows a contextual menu:

```
public IActionResult Index()
{                          ▣  Add View...
    return View();
}                          💡 Quick Actions and R
```

Select `Add View` from the contextual menu and you're provided with a dialog :

At this point we can keep the "template" as "Empty (without model)". This is a feature we'll learn to use a bit later. Let's simply make sure the "Create as a partial view" checkbox is unchecked so that a full page is created. As far as the "Use a layout page" option is concerned, you already know what that means.

So let's click the Add button and let the magic happen. Visual Studio creates the view, and voilÃ . Here's the view that was created :

```
Action1.cshtml  ⚲ ✕  HomeController.cs        _ViewImport
  1
  2      @{
  3          ViewData["Title"] = "Action1";
  4      }
  5
  6      <h2>Action1</h2>
  7
  8
```

Quite empty, but Visual Studio just saved us some time. 2 minutes saved for each view, multiplied by 30 views for a medium-sized project: that sums up to an hour saved. Which means less time coding and more time having fun. And I'm yet to show you even more powerful time-savers. Time to grab a drink and celebrate !

6.5 Let's go all the way

Alright, we just created an action and a view. Let me add some code to show usage of the ViewBag. Or ViewData for those who prefer, it's just a matter of taste as you just learned. I'm going to display on my page the list of available languages.

In my controller action, I'll fetch the data and pass it to the view. Here's the code of my completed action :

```
public IActionResult Action1()
{
  var files = System.IO.Directory
    .GetFiles(@"c:\");
  ViewBag.FilesList = files; ← passes data

  return View();
}
```

Nothing complicated here. There is no `FilesList` property on the `ViewBag`, but the compiler will be just fine since it's declared as a dynamic object.

Let's code the view now. Going back to the Views/Home-/Action1.cshtml file I'll just write:

```
<h2>Files in
  <strong>@ViewBag.Directory</strong>:
</h2>

<ul>
  @foreach (var file in ViewBag.FilesList)
  {
    <li>@file</li>
  }
</ul>
```

Which renders (hit Ctrl-F5 while in the view) in our browser as :

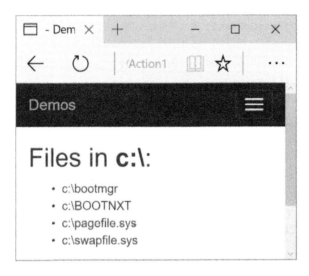

Let's just get things a bit further using a HTML helper (we saw that in the helpers section). We change the view to become :

```
@{
  var files = ViewBag.FilesList as string[];
  var listItems = files.Select(
    f => new SelectListItem() { Text = f }
  );
}

<h2>Files in
  <strong>@ViewBag.Directory</strong>:
</h2>

<div class="row">
```

```
<div class="col-xs-6">
  @Html.ListBox("lang", listItems)
</div>
<div class="col-xs-6">
  @Html.DropDownList("lang2", listItems)
</div>
</div>
```

Some things to note about that code :

- We use div elements like <div class="row"> and <div class="col-xs-6"> just for layout purposes. Those are Bootstap classes we saw earlier. They have nothing to do with ASP.NET MVC.
- I'd love to avoid the first line of the C# code block and simply write @Html.ListBox("lang", ViewBag.FilesList), since that would make things simpler. Unfortunately we can't since the ViewBag properties are not typed and the ListBox method has several overloads so the runtime compiler can't infer which one to call. Don't worry though, we're going to learn about typed models right now, which will allow us to avoid such casting code.

Here's the result :

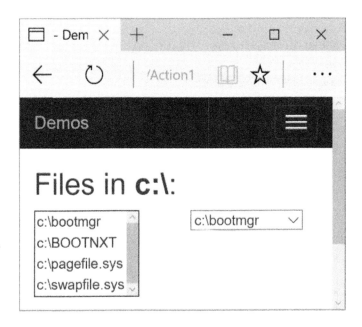

7. Typing things up

7.1 The problem with ViewBag and ViewData

Since `ViewData` and `ViewBag` properties are not typed, using them induces several problems :

- There is no check at compile-time that a property used in the view really is part of the `ViewData` or `ViewBag`.
- When typing the properties in the view, there is no Intellisense help from Visual Studio: we need to type them blindly.
- Before using the properties you'll need to cast them, which makes necessary the first awful line in our untyped ViewBag example.
- If we remove or rename properties of the `ViewBag` or change the type of the objects we place in it, the view won't be aware of the change, which will result in run-time errors.

7.2 Using and typing the model

Fortunately, there's a way to get compile-time checks, Intellisense and all of the nifty things we just wished we had: when returning a view, an action may provide it with a `model`. Here's how the action passes data :

```
return View(myData);
```

Once you do this, the view will be able to access that `myData` object through its `Model` property. But still, we won't be nicer-off than with a `ViewData` or `ViewBag`. Easy: since the `Model` property can be anything, it is initially typed as an `object`. But you can declare its type in the view using the `model` directive. Let's say that we pass a `MyTypes.SomeProduct` to a view. At the top of the view we may just write :

```
@model MyTypes.SomeProduct
```

Let's rewrite the preceding example using a typed model. Our controller becomes :

```
string directory = @"c:\";
var files = System.IO.Directory
    .GetFiles(directory);
ViewBag.Directory = directory;

return View(files);
```

and our view:

```
@model string[]
@{
  var listItems = Model.Select(
    f => new SelectListItem() { Text = f }
  );
}

<h2>Files in
  <strong>@ViewBag.Directory</strong>
</h2>

<div class="row">
  <div class="col-xs-6">
    @Html.ListBox("lang", listItems)
  </div>
  <div class="col-xs-6">
    @Html.DropDownList("lang2", listItems)
  </div>
</div>
```

It's a bit shorter, but most important we get :

- Intellisense support for our LINQ expression, including the selectable properties
- Compile-time check of any member from the model we use
- A cleaner code

7.3 Conventions and simplicity: introducing the ViewModel

Good things can even get better. When using a typed model, you may soon find yourself faced with other challenges :

- how do I pass several different objects to my view ?
- how do I gracefully handle a change of type in my model ?
- how can I make sure the type of my model stated at the top of my view is correct ?
- how can I transform my data into a displayable format (e.g. the `string[]` into a `IEnumerable<SelectListItem>`) without polluting the view or action ?

Those questions can simply be answered by creating a new class for each view: the *ViewModel*. You can name it according to the view, and it can have a property for each object you need to pass to the view.

Using a *ViewModel* is optional and pure convention. Just to make things straight we can adopt the following conventions :

- ViewModels are placed in a folder named *ViewModels*, in a subfolder named after the controller that normally leads to the view (just like `.cshtml` files in the Views folder).

- For a view named *MyView*, the ViewModel would be named *MyViewViewModel*.
- The ViewModel will have a property for each user input or output the view makes.

Let's create our languages sample again from scratch using a ViewModel approach. We first create a `ViewModels` folder and a `Home` subfolder:

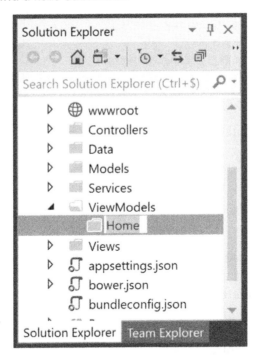

In the `ViewModels\Home\` folder we add a *ListFilesView-Model.cs* file declaring the following class :

```
using Microsoft.AspNetCore.Mvc.Rendering;
using System.Collections.Generic;
using System.Linq;

namespace Demos.ViewModels.Home
{
  public class ListFilesViewModel
  {
    public ListFilesViewModel(
      string directory, string[] files)
    {
      FilesList = files.Select(
        f => new SelectListItem() { Text = f }
      );
    }
    public IEnumerable<SelectListItem> FilesList
      { get; private set; }
    public string Directory
      { get; private set; }
  }
}
```

As you can see, our ViewModel converts the data fetched
by the controller into displayable data. That allows for
two architectural niceties :

- the view won't polluted with C# code
- the controller won't polluted with presentation-re-
  lated code.

That's fine architecture. Like any architecture, it isn't

strictly needed but in the long run it'll make things easier when we maintain that code over the years. Which means you could skip that ViewModel thing if you are writing quick garbage-prone code.

Let's add a `ListFiles` action to our Home controller :

```
public IActionResult ListFiles()
{
  string directory = @"c:\";
  var files = System.IO.Directory
    .GetFiles(directory);

  var vm = new ListFilesViewModel(
    directory,
    files
  );

  return View(vm);
}
```

For the view creation part, let's use Visual Studio to make things easier, again. Except this time we can tell Visual Studio about our ViewModel. We right-click the `ListFiles` action and select `Add View...` which pops up the "Add View" dialog. If we select `Details` in the `Template` field we can specify a `Model` class, and that's where we'll type in the name of our ViewModel :

Typing in the ViewModel just ensured that the generated view has a @model directive at its top. Not that much, but it avoids any error: we get IntelliSense to help in the dialog box.

Let's write the view using our ViewModel :

```
@model Demos.ViewModels.Home.ListFilesViewModel

<h2>
  Files in
  <strong>@Model.Directory</strong>
</h2>

<div class="row">
  <div class="col-xs-6">
    @Html.ListBox("lang", Model.FilesList)
  </div>
```

```
<div class="col-xs-6">
  @Html.DropDownList("lang2", Model.FilesList)
</div>
</div>
```

Not only do we get a neat view where C# is kept to its bare minimum, but while we type we notice IntelliSense kicks in to help: no more error nor wandering around like if we used the ViewBag, plus compile-time checks.

The final result is the same as before, but we now have solid, maintainable code we can be proud of. That's professional.

 Exercise This is a small exercise that is independent from the main exercises we are doing. Just to make sure you get some practice about what we just saw.

Add a FileSystemController controller with an action named Index. The Index action should return a view and provide that view with a list of files in the C:\ folder (or any folder you can give the application access to).

Create the Index view for the FileSystemController controller. That view should display the list of files in the aforementioned folder.

8. Dependency Injection (DI)

While not strictly necessary in an ASP.NET MVC application, dependency injection is an architecture pattern that solves several real-world problems.

The main idea behind dependency injection is inversion of concern (IoC): instead of creating object instances, your code simply ask for them. The actual process of creating those objects is delegated to a container.

That means that when you need a piece of functionality you just ask for it and use it. The actual functionality being created may be a singleton or not, and may differ from development to staging and production environments; that part is defined by you when configuring the container.

Setting up basic dependency injection in an ASP.NET MVC project is very simple. .NET core comes with a basic dependency injection system that should fit the needs of small projects. Should your project grow further, you can replace it with a DI framework that's better suited to your needs.

8.1 DI steps

Dependency injection is a two-step process:

What we call services are just plain .NET classes. Architecturally speaking, services should provide small pieces of functionality.

Let's see how those steps are done in code.

8.2 Services registration

Services that will be used are registered in the Configure-Services method of the Startup class.

Often there are several versions of a service and the actual version to be created depends on several factors like the environment. For instance, a logging service may simply log to the console in your development environment but will log to a logging service or through email once in production. That kind of problem is often solved in object oriented development using interfaces, so you are encouraged to write interfaces for your services.

Let's suppose that we have the following service interface and classes:

```
public interface IRequestLogger
{
  void Log(string message);
}

public class DevelopmentLoggerService
  : IRequestLogger
{
  public void Log(string message)
  {
    Console.WriteLine(message);
  }
}

public class ProductionLoggerService
  : IRequestLogger
{
  public void Log(string message)
  {
    // send to an external logging service
  }
}
```

Up to now, that's just traditional C# code. Registering this service is as simple as writing the following code in the Startup class:

```
public void ConfigureServices(
  IServiceCollection services)
{
  services.AddTransient<ILogger,
    DevelopmentLoggerService>();
}
```

That tells the DI system that whenever the ILogger service is requested, a new instance of DevelopmentLoggerService will be provided.

Now, using the basic DI system, you get three ways to have a service created:

- Transient creates a new instance of the service each time it is requested;
- Singleton will create the service only once and share it among everyone that uses it;
- Scoped will create a new instance of the service everytime a new HTTP request comes in, and will share it among all code that is invoked during the same HTTP request.

It would make sense to have the *DevelopmentLoggerService* created as a singleton for performance purposes, but have the *ProductionLoggerService* shared among a single HTTP request so that all of the information for a request is grouped together. Which means that a real world version of the Startup.ConfigureServices method could be:

```
if(Configuration.GetValue<bool>("consoleLog"))
{
  services.AddTransient<IRequestLogger,
    DevelopmentLoggerService>();
}
else
{
  services.AddScoped<IRequestLogger,
    ProductionLoggerService>();
}
```

In case you wonder about the Configuration property used in the first line, it's already there when using the default ASP.NET Core MVC template. It's just about getting configuration from the *appsettings.json* file. We'll learn more about configuration later in that book.

8.3 Getting services through injection

Now that the dependency injection system knows about your service, you can require them all through your application. The way you require them simply depends on where you are.

Requiring in a controller

```
public class ProductsController : Controller
{
   public ProductsController(IRequestLogger logger)
   {
     . . .
   }
}
```

Requiring in a controller action

```
public IActionResult ListServices(
   [FromServices] IRequestLogger logger)
{
   . . .
}
```

Requiring in a view

```
@inject IRequestLogger logger

<span>@logger.GetStatus()</span>
```

All in all, you can see that once your services are registered it's very easy to get them.

8.4 Extension methods for dependency injection

If you have a look at the rest of the ConfigureServices method, you'll find code such as:

```
services.AddMvc();
```

```
services.AddIdentity<ApplicationUser, IdentityRole>()
    .AddEntityFrameworkStores<ApplicationDbContext>()
    .AddDefaultTokenProviders();
```

Those don't use the AddTransient, AddScoped or AddSingleton methods. This is just good practice: most packages offer an extension method in the Microsoft.Extensions.Depende namespace that will configure all of their services, optionally taking some configuration information.

8.5 Wrapping it up

The *ListFiles* action we wrote earlier directly accesses the file system. That would make testing it difficult since the results would depend on the actual file system where the tests run. Also, since it directly calls the *Directory.GetFiles* it is dependent on the file system so we would need to change the code should we use e.g. a cloud storage for production. Let's fix that using dependency injection.

First, let's create the service in a new *FileStorageService.cs* file in the *Services* folder. We'll use an interface just so that we are prepared for unit testing and the production cloud storage.

```
public interface IFileStorage
{
  void ChangeDirectory(string directory);
  string[] GetCurrentFiles();
}

public class FileStorageService : IFileStorage
{
  string directory;
  public void ChangeDirectory(string directory)
  {
    this.directory = directory;
  }

  public string[] GetCurrentFiles()
  {
    return System.IO.Directory
      .GetFiles(directory);
  }
}
```

Now we can request that service in a controller and use it in an action:

```
public class HomeController : Controller
{
  IFileStorage fileStorage;
  public HomeController(IFileStorage fileStorage)
  {
    this.fileStorage = fileStorage;
  }

  public IActionResult ListFiles()
  {
    string directory = @"c:\";

    fileStorage.ChangeDirectory(directory);
    var files = fileStorage.GetCurrentFiles();

    var vm = new ListFilesViewModel(
      directory,
      files
    );

    return View(vm);
  }
}
```

As such, our code would result in an error: we need to instruct the DI system about how an instance of IFileStorage should be created. So we add the following code to the Startup.ConfigureServices method:

```
public void ConfigureServices(
  IServiceCollection services)
{
  services.AddTransient<IFileStorage,
    FileStorageService>();
}
```

That's it ! Our code got more complex, but that makes it testable and future-proof. Two nice qualities of enterprise-grade software.

9. Entity Framework Core models

Being familiar with .NET, you know by now that Visual Studio and the .NET Framework are excellent productivity tools that help you build data-driven applications in no time. You'll be glad to know that Visual Studio provides good support for Entity Framework within ASP.NET MVC.

Just in case you aren't familiar with Entity Framework, I'm going to quickly explain how to get running using Entity Framework Code First.

Entity Framework provides object-relational mapping. That is, it can save you the hassle of writing most of your data-access code. It is based on providers that actually handle the data access like *InMemory* (for testing purposes) or *SqlServer*.

In the simplest scenario, we code one class for each table in a database. Let's code a Car class :

```
public class Car
{
  public int ID { get; set; }
  public string Model { get; set; }
  public double MaxSpeed { get; set; }
}
```

In order to access a database we need a *context* class. A class on which to we call methods that get and update the data from the database. Such classes are typically named *CarFactory* or *DataFactory*, or even *DataAccess*.

Easily done using Entity Framework: all we have to do is inherit from the DbContext class and add one property for each table, typed as DbSet<T>. In our example that would be :

```
public class GarageFactory : DbContext
{
    public DbSet<Car> Cars { get; set; }
    // add any other table here
}
```

Since our MVC application gets its services injected, let's ensure a *GarageFactory* instance will be available for controllers that need data access. This needs two steps:

1. add a constructor to *GarageFactory* class that gets options ;
2. register *GarageFactory* during dependency injection setup, that is in Startup.ConfigureServices.

Here is the overloaded constructor we need to add, even if empty:

```
public class GarageFactory : DbContext
{
  public GarageFactory
    DbContextOptions<GarageFactory> options)
  : base(options) { }

    public DbSet<Car> Cars { get; set; }
}
```

And here is the code to be added to the Startup.ConfigureServices method:

```
services.AddDbContext<GarageFactory>(
  options => options.UseSqlServer(
    Configuration.GetConnectionString(
      "DefaultConnection")
));
```

The code above assumes that a connection string is defined in your configuration file (more about configuration later) and named "DefaultConnection".

No problem about that: when using the default template with user account authentication the following line was added to the appsettings.json file:

```
{
  "ConnectionStrings": {
    "DefaultConnection":
      "Server=(localdb)\\mssqllocaldb;Database=..."
  },
  ...
}
```

We're almost there! Now we could manually create a database, but we can get Entity Framework to do this for us using pure C# code. For real deployments we would need an advanced system and Entity Framework provides *migrations* for that purpose. For our purpose I'll just go on with a quick and dirty solution: an explicit creation of a *Car* row if there is none.

Let's create an initializer service:

```
public class GarageInitializer
{
  GarageFactory context;
  public GarageInitializer(
    GarageFactory context)
  {
    this.context = context;
  }

  public void Initialize()
  {
    context.Database.EnsureCreated();
```

```
    if (context.Cars.Any()) { return; }

    context.Cars.Add(new Car() {
      MaxSpeed = 100,
      Model = "Good old car"
    });
    context.Cars.Add(new Car() {
      MaxSpeed = 150,
      Model = "Premium car"
    });
    context.Cars.Add(new Car() {
      MaxSpeed = 190,
      Model = "Luxury car"
    });
    context.SaveChanges();
  }
}
```

In order to make that service available to controllers, I'll just add it to the DI container in the Startup.ConfigureServices method:

```
public class Startup
{
  public void ConfigureServices(
    IServiceCollection services)
  {
    ...
    services.AddTransient<GarageInitializer,
      GarageInitializer>();
  }
}
```

Now, Visual Studio can generate the necessary controller, actions and views for a full CRUD scenario in no time. We'll see that in a moment, but for now we'll manually code an action and view that display a list of cars, plus the fastest car. Though it's not necessary, we'll use a View-Model so that we can brag about our great architecture.

Suppose we want to display the list of cars, and details about the fastest one. Let's add a ViewModel, much like the ShowLanguagesViewModel we added earlier :

```
public class CarsListViewModel
{
  public CarsListViewModel(IEnumerable<Car> cars)
  {
    CarsList = cars.Select(
      c => new SelectListItem() { Text = c.Model }
    );
    FastestCar = cars
      .OrderByDescending(c => c.MaxSpeed)
```

```
    .FirstOrDefault();
  }

  public IEnumerable<SelectListItem>
    CarsList { get; private set; }
  public Car FastestCar { get; set; }
}
```

Note we compute the fastest car here, but we might as well decide to compute it in the controller.

Let's add a controller and action :

```
public class GarageController : Controller
{
  GarageFactory factory;
  GarageInitializer initializer;

  public GarageController(
    GarageFactory factory,
    GarageInitializer initializer)
  {
    this.factory = factory;
    this.initializer = initializer;
  }

  public IActionResult CarsList()
  {
    initializer.Initialize();
    var viewModel = new CarsListViewModel(
      factory.Cars);
```

```
    return View(viewModel);
  }
}
```

Note that since GarageFactory and GarageInitializer were added as services, I simply as for them in my constructor.

Let's finally add our view. Remember the easy way? Yes, we right-click the action, select Add View..., and fill the dialog.

It's plain easy to write the view thanks to the ViewModel and IntelliSense :

```
@model Demos.ViewModels.CarsListViewModel

<h2>All cars</h2>
@Html.ListBox("carsList", Model.CarsList)

<h2>Fastest car</h2>
<dl>
  <dt>ID</dt>
  <dd>@Model.FastestCar.ID</dd>
  <dt>Model</dt>
  <dd>@Model.FastestCar.Model</dd>
  <dt>Max speed</dt>
  <dd>@Model.FastestCar.MaxSpeed</dd>
</dl>
```

And here's the result :

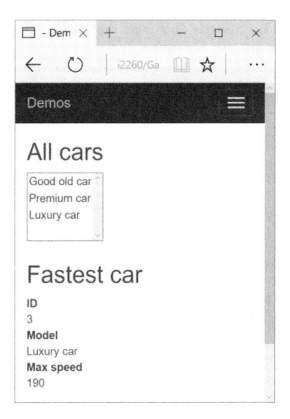

We can have a look at the database that was created. It's a local SQL Server database containing the Car table and two lines created by our GarageInitializer class.

Let's open the *Server Explorer* window, right-click the *Data connections* node and select *Add connection....* In the dialog I'll set (localdb)\mssqllocaldb as the server name (the one that's in appsettings.json) and select the right database (this is also in appsettings.json).

Now we can see the *Cars* table that was created in the database and its contents :

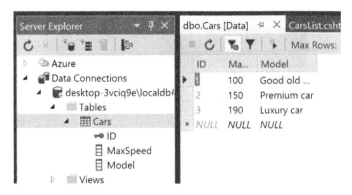

Entity Framework goes beyond the scope of this book, however it's good to note that a few lines of code have the ability to create a database and access it. Entity Framework hides all the complexity and SQL queries.

Moreover, we're not limited to a local file. Remember the connection string in appsettings.json ? When the need comes to connect to a full-size SQL Server database, all we need to do is change the connection string. Neat.

I'm sure by now you're more than longing for some coding. Time has come.

9.1 Exercise - Create the Product model and DbContext

 Our Web site is an e-commerce application, meaning we need to store products. We'll store them in a database. And we'll access the database using *Code First* Entity Framework.

You must add a Product class and an Entity Framework context class.

Make sure you declare the following properties in the Product class : ID: int Name: string Description: string Price: decimal ImageName: string

You must also add a class named ShopDbContext that inherits from the Entity Framework DbContext class, and provides access to a list of Product objects coming from the Product table of a database.

Make sure you register the ShopDbContext context with the dependency injection system in the ConfigureServices method of the Startup class.

9.2 Exercise solution

- In the Solution Explorer, right-click the Models folder and select Add / Class ... from the contextual menu.

- In the Add New Item dialog box, type Product in the Name input field. Click the OK button.
- In the Product.cs file, locate the following code :

```
public class Product
{

}
```

- Replace it with the following one :

```
public class Product
{
    public int ID { get; set; }
    public string Name { get; set; }
    public string Description { get; set; }
    public decimal Price { get; set; }
    public string ImageName { get; set; }
}
```

- In the Solution Explorer, right-click the Data folder and select Add / Class ... from the contextual menu.
- In the Add New Item dialog box, type ShopDbContext in the Name input field. Click the OK button.
- At the top of the ShopDbContext.cs file, add the following using statements :

```
using Microsoft.EntityFrameworkCore;
using MyShop.Models;
```

- In the `ShopDbContext.cs` file, locate the following code :

```
public class ShopDbContext
{

}
```

- Replace it with the following one :

```
public class ShopDbContext : DbContext
{
  public ShopDbContext(
    DbContextOptions<ShopDbContext> options)
    : base(options)
  {

  }

  public DbSet<Product> Products { get; set; }
}
```

- Using the Solution Explorer, open the `Startup.cs` file and add the following lines anywhere in the `ConfigureServices` method :

```
services.AddDbContext<ShopDbContext>(options =>
  options.UseSqlServer(
    Configuration.GetConnectionString(
      "DefaultConnection")));
```

9.3 Exercise - Add code that creates a database with some products

 In order to seed the database with some initial data, add an IShopInitializer interface with a Initialize method. The Initialize method takes no parameter and returns no value.

Add a class called ShopInitializer that implements the IShopInitializer interface. The Initialize method should ensure that the database exists and create some products when there is none.

Make sure that the ShopInitializer class is declared as a transient service in the Startup.ConfigureServices method.

In the Startup.Configure method, request an instance of IShopInitializer and call its Initialize method.

9.4 Exercise solution

- In the Solution Explorer view, right-click the *Services* folder and select *Add* then *New item....*

- In the *Add New Item* dialog, select *Interface* and type IShopInitializer in the *Name* field. Click the *Add* button.
- Replace the scaffolded interface definition with the following one:

```
public interface IShopInitializer
{
  void Initialize();
}
```

- In the Solution Explorer view, right-click the *Services* folder and select *Add* then *Class....*
- In the *Add New Item* dialog, type ShopInitializer in the *Name* field. Click the *Add* button.
- Replace the scaffolded interface definition with the following one:

```
public class ShopInitializer : IShopInitializer
{
  ShopDbContext shopContext;
  public ShopInitializer(ShopDbContext shopContext)
  {
    this.shopContext = shopContext;
  }
  public void Initialize()
  {
    shopContext.Database.EnsureDeleted();
```

```
shopContext.Database.EnsureCreated();

if (shopContext.Products.Any())
{
  return;
}

shopContext.Products.Add(
  new Product() {
    Name = "Yoghurt",
    Description = "Its freshness will melt you.",
    Price = 3.5M
  });
shopContext.Products.Add(
  new Product() {
    Name = "Banana",
    Description = "Great for a snack.",
    Price = 1.2M
  });
  shopContext.SaveChanges();
  }
}
```

 The `EnsureDeleted()` call should be removed once the application is over. We're going to need it when we add pictures to our database, but you can remove it afterwared. A proper way to handle such schema changes would be to use *data migrations*.

- Using the Solution Explorer, open the Startup.cs file and add the following lines anywhere in the ConfigureServices method :

```
services.AddTransient<
  IShopInitializer,
  ShopInitializer>();
```

- Still in the Startup.cs file, locate the Configure method. Add the following parameter to it :

```
IShopInitializer shopInitializer
```

- Add the following code at the end of the Configure method :

```
shopInitializer.Initialize();
```

9.5 Exercise - Display a products list

 You must modify the Home/Index view so that it displays 10 products from the database, ordered by product name.

Here's the result you should get

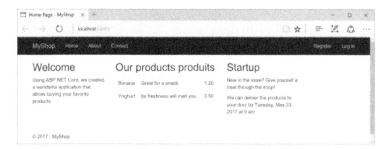

9.6 Exercise solution

- In the Solution Explorer, open the Controllers / HomeController.cs file.
- In the HomeController.cs file, locate the following code :

```
public IActionResult Index()
{
  return View();
}
```

- Replace it with the following one :

```
public IActionResult Index(
  [FromServices] ShopDbContext shopContext)
{
  var products = shopContext.Products
    .OrderBy(p => p.Name)
    .Take(10);
  return View(products);
}
```

- In the Solution Explorer, open the Views / Home / Index.cshtml file.
- In the Index.cshtml file, locate the following code :

```
<div class="col-md-3">
  <h2>Welcome</h2>
  . . .
</div>
<div class="col-md-3">
  <h2>Startup</h2>
  . . .
</div>
```

- Replace it with the following one :

```
<div class="col-md-3">
  <h2>Welcome</h2>
  . . .
</div>
<div class="col-md-4">
  <h2>Our products</h2>

  <table class="table table-striped">
    @foreach (var product in Model)
    {
      <tr>
        <td>@product.Name</td>
        <td>@product.Description</td>
        <td>@product.Price</td>
      </tr>
    }
  </table>
</div>
<div class="col-md-3">
```

```
<h2>Startup</h2>
  ...
</div>
```

- Click the Build / Build Solution menu.
- Run the application: click the Debug / Start Debugging menu.

10. Updating server data

10.1 Action parameters

When updating server data, you need to pass information from the browser to your application. This is simply handled by the routing system which will call your actions with parameters.

Let's look again at the default route in the `Startup` class

```
routes.MapRoute(...,
    template: "{controller=Home}/{action=Index}/{id?}")
```

Note the {id?} part? It means that anything coming after the action name (and separated from it by a slash sign) will be considered as an `id` parameter. The question mark states that this parameter is optional.

In order to get this parameter, all you have to do is add a parameter with the same name to you action method. For instance :

```
public class ProductsController : Controller
{
  public IActionResult Action1(string id)
  { ... }
}
```

Considering the default route, this action can be called simply by typing the following URL :

```
http://site/products/action1/abcd
```

In that case, our `ProductsController.Action1` method will be invoked with a value of `abcd` for its `id` parameter.

We could add as many parameters as needed to our action and modify the route accordingly. Needless to say that parameters should be short, since they add up to the URL length.

> As far as the type of the parameter is concerned (here we used `string`), ASP.NET MVC gracefully handles any conversion. So we could have declared our action with an `id` parameter of type `int` for instance. Of course, `abcd` would be rejected if we did so.

Whatever happens, we can also pass action parameters using standard URL query parameters. Consider for instance the following action :

```
public class ProductsController : Controller
{
  public IActionResult Rename(int id, string newName)
  { ... }
}
```

In order to invoke it with an id value of 15 and a newName value of sandwich, we can simply use the following URL

```
http://site/products/rename/15?name=sandwich
```

Note that sandwich is passed as a query parameter since it's not part of the route definition. We could also modify the route definition - or add a new one - in order to make it part of the URL.

10.2 Word of caution about URLs

As we saw earlier, route definitions may change later, for instance in order to improve SEO or provide user-friendly URLs. Which means it's important not to rely on them in your views.

The following view code will break if the route change, so avoid using it :

```
@* bad *@
<a href="/home/index/3">Some page</a>
```

Instead, you should prefer :

```
@* good *@
@Html.ActionLink("Some page",
  "Index", "Home", new { id=3 }, null)
```

or even :

```
@* good *@
<a href="@Url.Action(
  "Index", "Home", new { id=3 })">Some page</a>
```

or still :

```
@* good *@
<a asp-controller="Home" asp-action="Index"
  asp-route-id="@id">Some page</a>
```

10.3 Exercise - Display product details

You must modify the Home/Index view
so a *Details* link is displayed next
to each product like in the following
screenshot :

Now, make sure that when the user
click the *Details* link she is taken
to a new *Details* view displaying the
clicked product details like the following one :

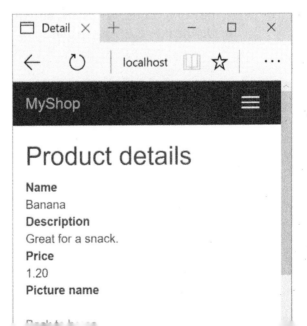

10.4 Exercise solution

- In the Solution Explorer, open the *Views / Home / Index.cshtml* file.
- In the *Index.cshtml* file, locate the following code :

```
<td>@product.Price</td>
```

- Replace it with the following one :

```
<td>@product.Price</td>
<td><a asp-action="Detail"
  asp-route-id="@product.ID">Details</a></td>
```

- In the Solution Explorer, open the *Controllers / HomeController.cs* file.
- In the *HomeController.cs* file, add the following method inside the HomeController class :

```
public IActionResult Detail(
  [FromServices] ShopDbContext shopContext,
  int id)
{
  var found = shopContext.Products
    .Where(p => p.ID == id)
    .FirstOrDefault();
  return View(found);
}
```

- Right-click the `Detail` method. From the contextual menu, select `Add View ....`
- In the `Add View` dialog, enter the following values :
- View name: Detail
- Template: Details
- Model class: Product (whatever your namespace here)
- Data context class: (leave empty)
- Click the `Add` button of the `Add View` dialog. That generates the *Views/Home/Detail.cshtml* view file.
- Click the *Build / Build Solution* menu.
- Run the application: click the *Debug / Start Debugging* menu.

10.5 HTTP Post parameters

Providing action parameters through the URLs is a good fit for short parameters that can be shown to the user. In case you want to pass longer action parameters or hide them from the URL, you can pass them as form data. It's almost as simple.

The view should declare a form in order to have the parameters sent :

```
<form method="post">
  First Name: <input name="firstname" type="text" />
  <input type="submit" />
</form>
```

> Of course we're not limited to the POST verb. You can use other HTTP verbs when you see fit.

In order to get the parameter, all that our view needs to to is declare a parameter with the same name :

```
public class ProductsController : Controller
{
  [HttpPost]
  public IActionResult Action1(string firstname)
  { ... }
}
```

Note the [HttpPost] attribute attached to the action method. By default, an action only reacts to HTTP GET requests, that's why we need it for a HTTP POST.

Now, if you want ASP.NET MVC to generate part of your form, you can use an HTML helper. Our view above would become

```
@using (Html.BeginForm())
{
    <input name="firstname" type="text" />
    <input type="submit" />
}
```

The same would go for the HTML input field and submit.

10.6 Passing a full blown object

ASP.NET MVC can make your job easy when you need to update full objects. Let's suppose you created a `Person` class :

```
public class Person
{
    public string FirstName { get; set; }
    public string LastName { get; set; }
}
```

You can write an action that takes a `Person` object as a parameter :

```
public class PersonController : Controller
{
  [HttpPost]
  public IActionResult CreatePerson(Person p)
  { ... }
}
```

All you need to do is to make sure that the incoming HTTP request contains parameters whose names match the properties declared in the Person class. ASP.NET will create a Person instance and pass it to your action.

For instance, we could write the following matching view :

```
@using (Html.BeginForm("CreatePerson", "Person"))
{
    <input name="firstname" type="text" />
    <input name="lastname" type="text" />
    <input type="submit" />
}
```

ASP.NET Core also comes with tag helpers, another way to enhance your HTML, in case the view Model is typed. So instead of using the Html.BeginForm HTML helper you could write the view as:

```
<form asp-action="CreatePerson" method="post">
  <input asp-for="FirstName" />
  <input asp-for="LastName" />
  <input type="submit" />
</form>
```

Note the **asp-** attributes in the view code above. Those are the tag helpers, and they will result in the HTML output being put on steroids. You can also write your own tag helpers.

10.7 Sit and watch - Basic product calculator

Let's begin with a simple example. I want to create a page that allows users to compute the product of two numbers. Easy. I'll first write a ViewModel class :

```
public class ComputeProductViewModel
{
    public ComputeProductViewModel(decimal? number1, \
decimal? number2)
    {
        Number1 = number1 ?? 0;
        Number2 = number2 ?? 0;
        Result = Number1 * Number2;
    }

    public decimal Number1 { get; private set; }
```

```
public decimal Number2 { get; private set; }
public decimal Result { get; set; }
}
```

As seen earlier, a ViewModel can have properties for everything that is input by and output to the user.

> For such a simple example, a ViewModel is simply overkill and we could easily do without. Nonetheless I encourage you to work with ViewModels in simple cases, so that it becomes a straightforward way to do for you. When more complex views come in your way, you'll simply apply the same techniques and go on seamlessly.

I'll then add a ComputeProduct action method to my Home controller. Note that it takes two parameters: the numbers to multiply :

```
public class HomeController : Controller
{
  public IActionResult ComputeProduct(
    decimal? number1, decimal? number2)
  {
    var viewModel = new ComputeProductViewModel(
      number1, number2);
    return View(viewModel);
  }
}
```

Now I'll right-click the `ComputeProduct` method and select `Add View...` from the contextual menu, then select an *Empty* template.

As my view code I'll type :

```
@model Demos.ViewModels.Home.ComputeProductViewModel

<h2>Product of two numbers</h2>

@using (Html.BeginForm())
{
    @Html.TextBoxFor(m => m.Number1)
    @Html.TextBoxFor(m => m.Number2)
    <input type="submit" value="Compute" />
}

<label>Result: @Html.DisplayFor(m=>m.Result)</label>
```

Not much new here, except for the use of two HTML helpers

- Html.TextBoxFor generates an input field for a given model member
- Html.Diplay generates a display element for a given model member

Both come in very handy since they take a lambda expression that provides your model and expects the member for with to generate the HTML element. Since we have a

typed model thanks to the @model directive, it's plain easy
to type thanks to IntelliSense and C# type-inference. Try
it in your own Visual Studio and you'll be surprised how
streamlined the experience is.

Let's run our view (Debug / Start Without Debugging menu).
We get the following result in our browser :

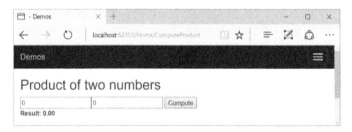

Of course, if works. When we input some numbers and
click the Compute button, we get our result :

It works. No surprise. Just one more thing: remember we
can provide action parameters using URL query parameters? It works here too. If we call our calculator view
using the following URL :

```
http://localhost:58599/Home/ComputeProduct?number1=5.\
2&number2=8
```

...we get the following result without event clicking the Compute **button (notice the URL) :**

10.8 Exercise - Add a search box to the products list

You must modify the Home/Index view: add a textbox input and a button that allows the user to search products typing a part of their name. Search results must appear in the existing list, showing only the top 10 ordered by name. The result looks like :

10.9 Exercise solution

- In the Solution Explorer, open the Controllers / HomeController.cs file.
- In the HomeController.cs file, locate the following code :

```
public IActionResult Index(
    [FromServices] ShopDbContext shopContext)
{
    var products = shopContext.Products
        .OrderBy(p => p.Name)
        .Take(10);
    return View(products);
}
```

- Replace it with the following one :

```
public IActionResult Index(
    [FromServices] ShopDbContext shopContext,
    string searchString)
{
    var products = shopContext.Products
        .Where(p =>
            string.IsNullOrEmpty(searchString)
            || p.Name.Contains(searchString))
        .OrderBy(p => p.Name)
        .Take(10);
    return View(products);
}
```

- In the Solution Explorer, open the Views / Home / Index.cshtml file.
- In the Index.cshtml file, locate the following code :

```
<div class="col-md-4">
  <h2>Our products</h2>
```

- Replace it with the following one :

```
<div class="col-md-4">
  <h2>Our products</h2>
  <form asp-action="Index">
    <input name="searchString" type="text" />
    <input type="submit" value="Search" />
  </form>
```

- Click the Build / Build Solution menu.
- Run the application: click the Debug / Start Debugging menu.

11. Updating data scenario

11.1 Steps

Now we need to support data input in a real-world scenario, not just sending some partial data. When you input data in a Web application, you do so through an HTML form. In fact, that process can be broken in two steps, whatever the server-side technology

HTTP GET
• User receives an input form

HTTP POST
• User sends new data and receives input form populated with sent data

11.2 Controller

Those two steps mean rendering a view twice, once for HTTP GET and once for HTTP POST. Which in turn means two actions inside our controller. Your controller would typically look like :

```
public class ProductsController : Controller
{
  public IActionResult Edit(int id)
  {
    ... // fetch data from data source
  }

  [HttpPost]
  public IActionResult Edit(int id, Product p)
  {
    ... // update the data source
  }
}
```

When the data source update is successful, you probably don't want the user to remain on the data input form. Which means the POST action would most likely contain a redirect statement. There is a RedirectToAction method for this on the base Controller class. It comes in handy since we provide the name of the action we want to redirect to :

```
[HttpPost]
public ActionResult Edit(int id, Product p)
{
  // ...
  if(successful) {
    return RedirectToAction("Index");
  }
}
```

11.3 Automated generation of controller and views

Now is time for me to show you a gem. In case we use Entity Framework as a data access layer, Visual Studio can generate in a breeze the controller, actions and views needed for a full CRUD scenario. What's more, the generated code isn't scary and can be modified to fit your needs.

Let's see how it works. Remember we have the following model that we wrote a while ago :

```
public class Car
{
  public int ID { get; set; }
  public string Model { get; set; }
  public double MaxSpeed { get; set; }
}
public class GarageFactory : DbContext
{
  public DbSet<Car> Cars { get; set; }
  // ...
}
```

All I have to do is right-click the `Controllers` directory in `Solution Explorer` and select `Add / Controller...` from the contextual menu :

In the `Add Scaffold` dialog box I select "MVC Controller with views, using Entity Framework" and click the `Add` button :

That gets me another dialog box, Add Controller, which I'll fill in the following way :

- Model class: Car
- Data context class: GarageFactory
- Generate views: checked (default value)

I'll leave the rest of the options to their default values. Here's the dialog box before I press the Add button :

That's all there is to it! I now have full actions and views for each CRUD operation.

Let's go for instance to the list of cars. We type the `http://localhost:62260/Cars` URL in our browser and get a nice list :

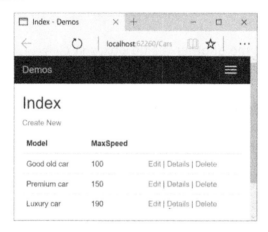

What's more, there are links to create, edit, delete and details views, all working. Time to get the paycheck and go surfing for the next week.

> Think you cannot use this wizard in real-life? Think again: if you look at the generated actions and views, they are concise and can be easily modified. Nothing is hidden from you. This is a real time-saver, no strings attached.

Well, I can feel that your fingers are getting itchy again. You want to try this by yourself? Great, that's just what we're about to do!

11.4 Exercise - Create the products management back-office

 You must now cater for the shop products management by the shopkeepers. You are to add the necessary pages. For now, they are open for public access, but don't worry: we'll change that later. Anyway, our application isn't published yet.

Add pages that allow to :

- list all of the products from the database (and add a link to that page in the site top menu);
- add a product to the database;
- edit a product in the database;
- delete a product from a database.

11.5 Exercise solution - Create the products management back-office

- Open the Views/Shared/_Layout.cshtml file.

- Locate the following code :

```
<li><a asp-area="" asp-controller="Home"
 asp-action="Index">Home</a></li>
```

- Replace it with the following one :

```
<li><a asp-area="" asp-controller="Home"
 asp-action="Index">Home</a></li>
<li><a asp-area="" asp-controller="Products"
 asp-action="Index">Manage products</a></li>
```

- In the Solution Explorer, right-click the `Controllers` folder and select Add / Controller ... from the contextual menu.
- In the Add Scaffold dialog, select "MVC Controller with views, using Entity Framework", then click the Add button.
- In the Add Controller dialog, enter the following values :

1. Model Class: Product (whatever your namespace here)
2. Data context class: ShopDbContext (whatever your namespace here)
3. Generate views: checked
4. Use a layout page: checked, leave the textbox below empty

5. Controller name: ProductsController

- Click the Add button of the Add Controller dialog and wait for the scaffolding to complete.
- Click the Build / Build Solution menu.
- Run the application: click the Debug / Start Debugging menu.

12. Doing more with controllers and actions

12.1 Actions can generate more than views

Since HTML is king in a Web application, we focused on the most common process where an action renders a view. However an action can generate anything that can be returned over HTTP. Basically, an action's output is to provide an HTTP response, and it doesn't have to be HTML.

That means our schema of a route / controller / action process has to be slightly modified. It becomes :

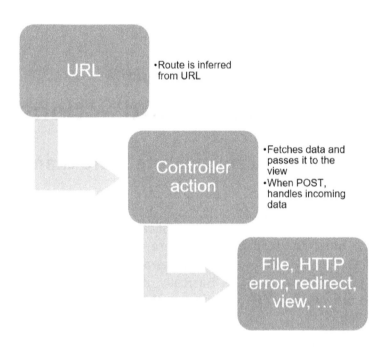

That's what the IActionResult interface is for. When we introduced actions and their ActionResult return type we mentioned that an action can return more than a view. IActionResult is an interface that many types implement. To name a few :

- ContentResult
- FileContentResult
- JsonResult
- NotFoundResult
- NoContentResult
- OkResult

- PartialViewResult
- PhysicalFileResult
- RedirectResult
- RedirectToActionResult
- RedirectToRouteResult
- UnauthorizedResult
- ViewResult

We already saw that we can generate a `ViewResult` by calling the `View` method from within our controller, and a `RedirectToRouteResult` calling the `RedirectToRoute` method. Following that pattern, a controller has plenty of simple methods to generate all these result types.

For instance, if we have a JPEG image contained in memory as a byte array, we can simply write :

```
public IActionResult Picture(int id)
{
  bool error = ...
  if (error)
  {
    return NotFound();
  }
  byte[] image = ...
  return File(image, "image/jpeg");
}
```

The picture action could then be invoked directly by a browser or referenced from an HTML `<img />` element. For instance you could type in a view

```
<img src="@Url.Action("Picture", "Home",
  new { id=3 })" />
```

Note that in the `Url.Action` helper, as in many helpers, you provide the parameters using an anonymous object. The `new { id=3 })` syntax allows you to pass in as many parameters as needed by the action. For instance, suppose my action were declared as :

```
public IActionResult Picture(
  int id, int width, int height)
{
  // ...
}
```

I could reference it from a view using the following syntax :

```
<img src="@Url.Action("Picture", "Home",
  new { id=3, width=100, height=50 })" />
```

12.2 Exercise - Add images to the products

 You must now:

- Create a folder named Images under the content folder. Add some images that represent the products you added to the database.
- Modify the home page products list: add an image next to each product description in the products list.

As a result, the home view should look like :

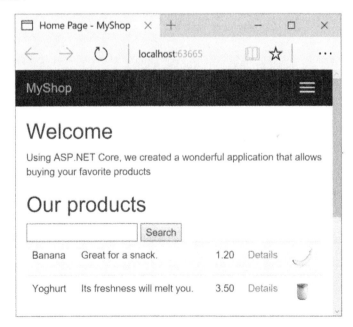

12.3 Exercise solution - Add images to the products

- In the Solution Explorer, right-click the `wwwroot` / `images` folder and select `Add / Existing item ...` from the contextual menu.
- Add 2 pictures. Let's suppose they are named "banana.jpg" and "yogurt.jpg".
- In the `Models\ShopFactory.cs` file, inside the `ShopInitializer` class, locate the following code :

```
shopContext.Products.Add(
  new Product()
  {
    Name = "Yoghurt",
    Description = "Its freshness will melt you.",
    Price = 3.5M
  });
shopContext.Products.Add(
  new Product()
  {
    Name = "Banana",
    Description = "Great for a snack.",
    Price = 1.2M
  });
```

- Replace it with the following one :

```
shopContext.Products.Add(
  new Product()
  {
    Name = "Yoghurt",
    ImageName = "yogurt.jpg",
    Description = "Its freshness will melt you.",
    Price = 3.5M
  });
shopContext.Products.Add(
  new Product()
  {
    Name = "Banana",
    ImageName = "banana.jpg",
    Description = "Great for a snack.",
    Price = 1.2M
  });
```

- In the `Controllers\HomeController.cs` file, inside the `HomeController` class, add the following method :

```
public IActionResult Image(
  [FromServices] ShopDbContext shopContext,
  int id)
{
  var found = shopContext
    .Products
    .Where(p => p.ID == id).FirstOrDefault();
  if (found == null)
  {
    return NotFound();
```

```
  }

  var fileName = string.Format(
    "~/images/{0}", found.ImageName);

  return File(fileName, "image/jpeg");
}
```

- Open the Views/Home/Index.cshtml file.
- Locate the following code

```
<td><a asp-action="Detail"
  asp-route-id="@product.ID">Details</a></td>
```

- Replace it with the following one :

```
<td><a asp-action="Detail"
  asp-route-id="@product.ID">Details</a></td>
<td><img src='@Url.Action("Image",
  new { id = product.ID })' height="30" /></td>
```

12.4 Input validation

When writing an application, part of your work as a developer is to make sure that data entered by the user is valid before processing it. Which means meeting several criteria. If you previously worked with data validation in UWP, WPF or Silverlight, you'll be glad to hear that ASP.NET MVC relies on the same code: it supports data annotations.

With data annotations, you simply use attributes and classes from the *System.ComponentModel.DataAnnotations* namespace to mark your model classes, and presentation layers use it to validate user input and provide feedback. That means you apply a nice coding principle: DRY (don't repeat yourself).

Let's say I want to ensure that when a car is created or modified, it meets the following business rules :

- MaxSpeed cannot be less that 10 or more than 300;
- Model must not be null or empty, and it must have at least 2 characters.

I can simply annotate the Car class using data annotation attributes :

```
using System.ComponentModel.DataAnnotations;

public class Car
{
  public int ID { get; set; }

  [Required]
  [RegularExpression("..+")]
  public string Model { get; set; }
```

```
[Range(10, 300)]
public double MaxSpeed { get; set; }
}
```

This is a simple example. For advanced data validation scenarios, you'll find that the *System.ComponentModel.DataAnnotation* namespace offers more attributes and classes that even allow you to provide your own validation code.

Then you have to make validation work. It's quite simple actually. On the controller side, inside the [HttpPost] action (or whatever action handles user-submitted data) you check for the ModelState.IsValid property. It will be automatically populated by the ModelBinder that injects the Car parameter into your action. You code could look like that :

```
[HttpPost]
public ActionResult Create(Car car)
{
  if (ModelState.IsValid)
  {
    // code that adds car to you data source
  }

  // remain on the same view so that the user
  // sees validation messages.
  return View(car);
}
```

On the view side, there are helpers that allow you to display your error messages. *Html.ValidationSummary* displays a list of all the error messages for that action, and *Html.ValidationMessageFor* displays errors for a specific property. A view code for the Create action could look like this :

```
@using (Html.BeginForm())
{
  @Html.ValidationSummary()

  @Html.EditorFor(
    model => model.Model)
  @Html.ValidationMessageFor(
    model => model.Model)

  @Html.EditorFor(
    model => model.MaxSpeed)
  @Html.ValidationMessageFor(
    model => model.MaxSpeed)
}
```

13. Basic security

Completely securing an ASP.NET Core application goes beyond the scope of this book. Much of it relies on techniques that are not specific of ASP.NET Core. There are however some basic steps you can take in order to prevent common attacks.

13.1 Preventing Cross-Site Scripting

Cross-Site Scripting, or XSS, is the technique where a hacker forces a victim's browser to make a request to your application. If you cannot detect XSS, that means your application may perform actions that were initiated without a user even knowing it. Which is bad if your site is about making money transfers, for instance.

A first rule of thumb is: never modify data based on a HTTP GET request. Rely on other adequate HTTP verbs for this, like POST or UPDATE. Second, a technique is to ensure that a user makes a GET request before initiating a POST or UPDATE request. Which is easily done using an anti-forgery token.

All you have to do is inject a hidden field in the page that renders to the user using the HTTP GET request, and check that this field is the same when the POST or UPDATE request comes in afterwards. Practically there are two steps to take in your code :

- In the view, call the Html.AntiForgeryToken() helper inside the form.
- On the POST or UPDATE action, add a ValidateAntiForgeryToken attribute.

 Instead of using *Html.AntiForgeryToken()* in the view, you can use tag helpers. Simply add an asp-action attribute to the form tag.

That's all there is to do. As a result, your view would look like :

```
@using (Html.BeginForm())
{
    @Html.AntiForgeryToken()
    ...
}
```

and your POST (or whatever) action :

```
[HttpPost]
[ValidateAntiForgeryToken]
public IActionResult Create(Car car)
{
    ...
}
```

13.2 Rejecting extra fields

Suppose your Car model has a Price property because this property may be read and modified from some secure part of the site. You however do not want anonymous users to change the price of a car. If you take a Car object as your action parameter, nothing stops a malicious user from hand-crafting a POST request containing a Price field. If you write your action as the following code, the Price property will be updated :

```
[HttpPost]
[ValidateAntiForgeryToken]
public IActionResult Create(Car car)
{
    ...
}
```

Not having a Property field in the view changes nothing: it's quite easy to hand-craft any POST request since it is pure text.

That's why you need to explicitly tell the ModelBinder which fields you expect in the POST request, for more security. This is done using the Bind attribute :

```
[HttpPost]
[ValidateAntiForgeryToken]
public IActionResult Create(
  [Bind(Include = "Model,MaxSpeed")] Car car)
{
  ...
}
```

That way, an incoming HTTP request cannot set the `Price` property of the `Car` object using that action.

13.3 Authenticating users

ASP.NET MVC has rich support for authentication. In fact, the application that Visual Studio scaffolded for us already takes care of identifying users.

If you look at the *Startup* class, you'll see the following code:

```
public void ConfigureServices(...)
{
  services
    .AddIdentity<ApplicationUser,IdentityRole>()
    .AddEntityFrameworkStores<ApplicationDbContext>()
    .AddDefaultTokenProviders();
}

public void Configure(...)
{
```

```
app.UseIdentity();
}
```

This code registers a basic authentication mechanism that uses a database as the underlying store. The `Appli-cationUser` class is a custom class that you can modify to fit your needs.

You could change that startup code and require other authentication mechanisms like OAuth.

Whatever the authentication provider you choose, there's a unified API to access it. From within your actions and views you can call the `User` property. Plus you get the `Authorize` attribute. Any action that you decorate with that attribute will reject unauthenticated users. If you prefer to reject roles or specific users, the `Authorize` attribute has properties for this.

13.4 Exercise - Secure the back-office

 Currently, any user may access the back-office. You must ensure that

- Users can register an account
- Users can log-in
- Only authenticated users may access the back-office

13.5 Exercise solution - Secure the back-office

- Open the *ControllersProductsController.cs* file.
- Locate the following code

```
public class ProductsController : Controller
```

- Replace it with the following one :

```
[Authorize]
public class ProductsController : Controller
```

14. State management

14.1 State stores

When an HTTP request comes through to your application, a controller instance is created in order to service it, then gets disposed. This means you cannot store local variables inside a controller.

Even if you created a singleton service, its data could not be considered persistent for two reasons:

1. the ASP.NET Core process may crash at any moment loosing such in-memory data;
2. once deployed you may need several instances of your ASP.NET Core in order to handle large workloads (load-balancing between them).

Persistent data is likely to be stored in a database (for instance using Entity Framework as we saw earlier) but there are more options from ASP.NET itself.

Here are some of your options:

What	Lifetime and visibility	Limits
Cache	All users, all pages	ASP.NET may remove data from the cache when memory gets scarce
Session	One user, all pages	Memory used = object size x sessions count
TempData	One user, all pages	Stored as cookies: only for non sensitive data
HttpContext.Ite ms	Single page, or pages linked by a Server.Transfer call	
QueryString	Pages linked by a hyperlink, a submitted form, or a redirect	

Among those, *Session* fits many uses. It is perfect for storing user-related temporary data like a shopping cart or data entered by a user across different pages.

14.2 Session state

Session has a limited lifetime because of the very nature of web applications. Since HTTP is a disconnected protocol, there is no straightforward way to know whether a user is looking at a page she got from you or if she left. So ASP.NET simply measures the time elapsed since the latest HTTP request. When that time goes beyond a certain timeout value, session data is removed from the server. Of course, the timeout duration may be changed as part of the session configuration.

Session data is stored on the server and a cookie with a session ID is assigned to the user in order to match her data.

In order to use sessions, you should:

- add the *Microsoft.AspNetCore.Session* NuGet package
- choose where the state is stored; for this you select an *IDistributedCache* implementation: in memory for simple needs but it can be Redis or SQL Server
- call *AddSession* and *UseSession* configuration methods from your *Startup* class.

An example configuration would be :

```
public class Startup
{
  public void ConfigureServices(
    IServiceCollection services)
  {
    ...
    services.AddDistributedMemoryCache();
    services.AddSession(options => {
      options.IdleTimeout = TimeSpan.FromMinutes(20);
      options.CookieHttpOnly = true;
    });
  }

  public void Configure(IApplicationBuilder app)
  {
    ...
    app.UseSession();
    ...
  }
}
```

Make sure that the *app.UseSession* line is above the *app.UseMvc* one. This is due to the fact that the middleware pipeline must have session ready before you can use it from an ASP.NET MVC component like a controller.

Now, from whatever part of the application you can read and write values to the session store using the current *HttpContext*. For this, you can request an *IHttpContextAccessor* instance. This is done thanks to dependency injection.

```
// request it using dependency injection
IHttpContextAccessor contextAccessor;

// writing a value
contextAccessor.HttpContext.Session
   .SetString(key, value);

// reading a value
string value = contextAccessor.HttpContext.Session
   .GetString(key);
```

14.3 Exercise - Add products to a basket

Next to each product, add an "Add to basket" link :

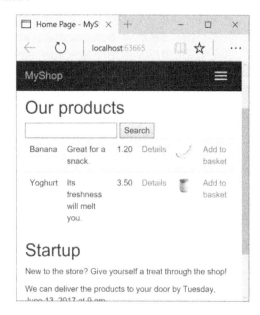

When a user clicks that link, the corresponding product must be added to a temporary basket that will be maintained across pages.

14.4 Exercise solution - Add products to a basket

- In the Solution Explorer, right-click the MyShop project and select *Manage NuGet Packages...* from the contextual menu.
- Make sur that the *Browse* tab is selected at the top.
- In the *Search* box located at the top, type *Microsoft.AspNetCore.Session*, select the result and click the *Install...* button.
- In the Solution Explorer, right-click the Services folder and select Add / Class ... from the contextual menu.
- Add a class named *BasketManager* with the following code :

```
public class BasketManager
{
  IHttpContextAccessor contextAccessor;
  ShopDbContext shopContext;

  public BasketManager(
    IHttpContextAccessor contextAccessor,
    ShopDbContext shopContext)
  {
    this.contextAccessor = contextAccessor;
    this.shopContext = shopContext;
  }
```

```
const string BASKET_KEY = "basket";
const char SEPARATOR = ',';
public void AddProduct(int id)
{
    var ids = GetIds();
    var newIds = ids.ToList();
    newIds.Add(id.ToString());
    string newIdsAsString = newIds.Aggregate(
        (a, b) => a + SEPARATOR + b);
    contextAccessor.HttpContext.Session
        .SetString(BASKET_KEY, newIdsAsString);
}


IEnumerable<string> GetIds()
{
    var current = contextAccessor.HttpContext.Session
        .GetString(BASKET_KEY);
    if (current == null)
    {
        return Enumerable.Empty<string>();
    }
    var ids = current.Split(SEPARATOR);
    return ids;
}
}
```

- In the Solution Explorer, right-click the Controllers folder and select Add / Controller ... from the contextual menu.
- In the *Add Scaffold* dialog box, select *MVC Con-*

troller - Empty and click the *Add* button.

- In the *Add Controller* dialog box, type BasketController as the name and click the *Add* button.
- Add the following code inside the BasketController class :

```
BasketManager basket;
public BasketController(BasketManager basket)
{
  this.basket = basket;
}

public IActionResult AddProduct(int id)
{
  basket.AddProduct(id);
  return RedirectToAction("Index", "Home");
}
```

- Add the following code to the ConfigureServices method of the Startup class :

```
services.AddSession(options =>
{
  options.IdleTimeout =
    TimeSpan.FromMinutes(20);
  options.CookieHttpOnly = true;
});
```

```
services.AddTransient<BasketManager>();
```

- In the `Configure` method of the `Startup` class locate the following code :

```
app.UseMvc(routes => ...);
```

- Replace it with the following one :

```
app.UseSession();
app.UseMvc(routes => ...);
```

- Add the following code to the `ConfigureServices` method of the `Startup` class :

```
services.AddTransient<BasketManager>();
```

- In the `Views\Home\Index.cshtml` file, locate the following code :

```
<tr>
  ...
  <td>
    <img src='@Url.Action("Image",
      new { id = product.ID })'
    height="30" />
  </td>
</tr>
```

- Replace it with the following one :

```
<tr>
  ...
  <td>
    <img src='@Url.Action("Image",
      new { id = product.ID })'
    height="30" />
  </td>
  <td>
    <a asp-action="AddProduct"
      asp-controller="Basket"
      asp-route-id="@product.ID">
        Add to basket
    </a>
  </td>
</tr>
```

14.5 Exercise - Basket contents

 Add a "View basket" link in the application header bar. When clicked, that link should display the basket contents :

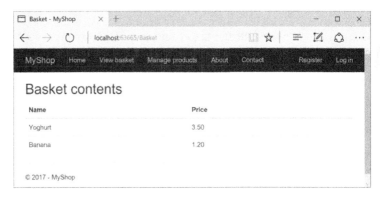

14.6 Exercise solution - Basket contents

- Add the following code to the `Services.BasketManager` class :

```
public IEnumerable<Product> GetProducts()
{
    var ids = GetIds();
    var products = shopContext.Products
      .Where(p => ids.Contains(p.ID.ToString()));
    return products;
}
```

- In the `Controllers\BasketController.cs` file, locate the following code :

```
public IActionResult Index()
{
  return View();
}
```

- Replace it with the following one :

```
public IActionResult Index()
{
  var contents = basket.GetProducts();
  return View(contents);
}
```

- In the `Views\Shared\_Layout.cshtml` file, locate the following code :

```
<li><a asp-area="" asp-controller="Home"
  asp-action="Index">Home</a></li>
```

- Replace it with the following one :

```
<li><a asp-area="" asp-controller="Home"
  asp-action="Index">Home</a></li>
<li><a asp-controller="Basket"
  asp-action="Index">View basket</a></li>
```

- In the `Controllers\BasketController.cs` file, right-click the `Index` method Add View... from the contextual menu.
- In the *Add View* dialog box, select an *Empty (without model)* template and click the *Add* button.
- Use the following code for the view that was just created :

```
@model IEnumerable<MyShop.Models.Product>

@{
    ViewData["Title"] = "Basket";
}

<h2>Basket contents</h2>

<table class="table">
  <thead>
```

```
  <tr>
    <th>Name</th>
    <th>Price</th>
    <th></th>
  </tr>
</thead>
<tbody>
  @foreach (var item in Model)
  {
    <tr>
      <td>
          @Html.DisplayFor(
            modelItem => item.Name)
      </td>
      <td>
          @Html.DisplayFor(
            modelItem => item.Price)
      </td>
    </tr>
  }
</tbody>
</table>
```

15. Web API

15.1 Use cases

There are mainly two use cases for creating an API.

Other clients

Up to now we created an HTML user interface. That's fine for consuming our application with a standard browser.

There may be other types of clients interested by your application data: mobile applications for iOS or Android devices, native Universal Windows applications, and in fact any type of standalone application.

Providing an API to them is just like providing them with a database access. The API will be available through HTTP, which means clients could connect through the internet or an intranet.

Client JavaScript frameworks

Popular JavaScript frameworks like Angular, React, Vue and Knockout have risen over the latest years. They enable for a rich in-browser user experience while simplifying the amount of code necessary for such applications.

Those applications typically make HTTP calls that are often REST/JSON to an API.

In fact, this is almost the same use case as before: the client will be a full-blown JavaScript/HTML application that runs inside the browser and makes AJAX calls to the API.

15.2 Creating an API is simple

Creating an API is as simple as writing actions inside a controller. In fact, it's just what we already learned except that there is no view. Which makes it even more simple.

Here is a basic API:

```
public class ValuesController : Controller
{
  [HttpGet]
  public MyResult Get()
  {
    ...
    return myResult;
  }
}
```

And here is a more complex one, giving you more control:

```
[Route("api/ProductsApi")]
public class ProductsApiController : Controller
{
  // GET: api/ProductsApi
  [HttpGet]
  public IEnumerable<Product> GetProducts()
  {
    return _context.Products;
  }

  // GET: api/ProductsApi/async
  [HttpGet("async")]
  public async Task<IActionResult> GetProductsAsync()
  {
    var products = await _context.Products
      .ToArrayAsync();
    return Ok(products);
  }
}
```

Note the use of a *HttpGetAttribute* attribute in order to specify the route you expect for that controller or actions.

In the above example, the second action is an asynchronous action so that our server can handle more simultaneous clients.

15.3 API results format

By default, the API we just wrote provides JSON results. Which is fine for many uses today. Should you need different formats, you can use auto-negociation.

Since clients send an "Accept" HTTP header, it can be used by ASP.NET Core in order to automatically adapt its response. For this negotiation to work, you just need to take two actions:

1. Add the NuGet packages for the formats you want to handle. They are named Microsoft. AspNetCore. Mvc. Formatters.*
2. From your actions, return *Ok(result)* instead of returning the result directly. For instance:

```
public class ValuesController : Controller
{
  [HttpGet]
  public MyResult Get()
  {
    ...
    return Ok(myResult);
  }
}
```

16. Going further

By now, you know the tools necessary to create an ASP.NET MVC application. You should be able to create your first application or site and learn by yourself.

When you are ready to progress further, this chapter gives you a few trails you may venture on.

16.1 Creating Razor helpers

Helpers allow you to factorize Razor code. If you liked the ones baked into ASP.NET MVC you sure will want to create your own.

It's easy: just declare your helper in a view, using Razor code :

```
@helper Remaining(DateTime date) {
    if (date < DateTime.Now)
    {
        <div>Finished.</div>
    }
    else
    {
        <div>Within @date.Subtract(DateTime.Now).Days d\
ays.</div>
    }
}
```

Then you may use that helper in the declaring view :

```
<div>@Remaining(Model.EndDate)</div>
```

Even better: if you declare your helper in a `TimeUtils.cshtml` file in the `App_Code` folder, you may use it from any view with the following syntax :

```
<div>@TimeUtils.Remaining(Model.EndDate)</div>
```

16.2 Display and edit templates

Suppose you use the `DisplayFor` helper :

```
@Html.DisplayFor(model => model.Product)
```

It asks ASP.NET MVC to render the `Product` property. In case that property is a `string` or another simple type, ASP.NET MVC will kind of just call the object's `ToString` method.

But what if the `Product` property is a complex type, one that you defined as a `ProductDetails` class? Well, it also works. All you have to do is provide a display template by adding a `ProductDetails.cshtml` file in the `Views/Shared/DisplayTemplates/` folder. That's neat, isn't it? Then you can code the `ProductDetails.cshtml` file just like it were a partial view. For instance, you could write :

```
@model ProductDetails

@if (Model != null)
{
    <div>Product: @Model.Name</div>
}
```

Neat, right? Best of all, you can do likewise for edit templates. Just use the `Html.EditorFor` helper, and place your file in the `Views/Shared/EditorTemplates/` folder. That's just the kind of nifty tricks that help me love ASP.NET MVC. How about you?

Definitions

Dynamic object

A dynamic object allows you to access properties (and other members) that are interpreted at run-time. It's a quite recent addition to the C# language that allows developers to code like if they were using VB.NET with `Strict=Off`.

In the following example, the last line wouldn't even compile if it weren't declared as a *dynamic* :

```
dynamic maListe = new List<Person>();
maListe.Add(new Person()); // compiles and runs corre\
ctly
maListe.Add(new Dog()); // compile but throws an exce\
ption at run-time
```

Entity Framework

An ORM framework included in the .NET Framework. Other examples of ORM frameworks include nHibernate or LINQ to SQL.

Project

A project represents all the files and actions needed to build an assembly (DLL or EXE). It appears as a folder tree containing files in the Solution Explorer.

It is stored on the disk as a `csproj` (for C#) or `.vbproj` (for VB.NET) file. It's an XML file that states which action to take on each file. Which is very handy when you need to build the project in a build factory.

Solution

A concept in Visual Studio that allows grouping of several projects.

On the disk, a solution is stored in a `.sln` file that simply contains a list of relative links to the projects it's made of.

This means that if necessary, you can create several solutions for a same application, which may be useful for large projects.

Solution Explorer

A window that shows a view of all the files in your solution, much like Windows Explorer. By default, it should be on the right-hand side of Visual Studio. If you cannot see it, use the menu `View / Solution Explorer`.

A word from the author

I sincerely hope you enjoyed reading this book as much as I liked writing it and that you quickly become proficient enough with ASP.NET Core.

If you would like to get in touch you can use :

- email: books@aweil.fr
- Facebook: https://facebook.com/learncollection

In case your project needs it, I'm also available for speaking, teaching, consulting and coding. All around the world.

If you liked this book, you probably saved a lot of time thanks to it. I'd be very grateful if you took some minutes of your precious time to leave a comment on the site where you purchased this book. Thanks a ton !

The Learn collection

This book is part of the *Learn collection*.

The *Learn collection* allows developers to self-teach new technologies in a matter of days.

Published books

- Learn ASP.NET Core MVC[1]
- Learn ASP.NET MVC[2]
- Learn Meteor[3]
- Learn WPF MVVM[4]

To be published

- Learn Xamarin
- Learn Universal Windows

---

[1] https://leanpub.com/netcore
[2] https://leanpub.com/aspnetmvc
[3] https://leanpub.com/learnmeteor
[4] https://leanpub.com/learnwpf

CPSIA information can be obtained
at www.ICGtesting.com
Printed in the USA
BVOW11s1914310817

493539BV00007B/141/P

9 780244 612344